Tanisha and Tamika's Toolbox
Linear Measurement Systems

Catherine Twomey Fosnot

Rebecca Murry

Sylvia Glassco

New Perspectives on Learning, LLC
1194 Ocean Avenue
New London, CT 06320

ISBN-13: 978-0-9976886-6-5

Table of Contents

Unit Overview 2

Day 1 – The Stanley FatMax 25 12
Students learn about Tanisha and Tamika's interest in tools and carpentry and measure out their own 25-foot measuring strip.

Day 2 – How Long is 25 Feet? 17
After a minilesson to encourage efficient conversion strategies, students share their strategies for measuring 25 feet and finding the equivalent number of yards and inches.

Day 3 – Tanisha's Tool Belt 24
After a quick minilesson, students ponder a 60-inch tape measure. How does it compare to 25 feet?

Day 4 – Which Measuring Tape is the Longest? 32
Students share their work finding the difference between the two lengths in a gallery walk and congress and end the day with a minilesson on addition and subtraction.

Day 5 – Plans for the Toolbox 37
Students add and subtract lengths in a minilesson, then make a plan for how to cut boards to construct a 4' x 3' x 2' toolbox.

Day 6 – Presenting the Plans 45
Students examine each other's work on the toolbox in a gallery walk and congress, then finish with another minilesson, adding and subtracting lengths.

Day 7 – A New Tool 48
A minilesson provides students an opportunity to discuss addition and subtraction strategies using an open number line. Next, students investigate the difference in length between a meter and 4 feet.

Day 8 – What's the Difference? 55
A minilesson and gallery walk prepare students to discuss their comparisons of centimeters and feet in a subsequent math congress.

Day 9 – About How Long? 60
Students estimate the length of objects around the classroom, discussing which unit would be best for each and finding the exact measurements.

Day 10 – More Measurements and A Learning Wall 64
Students share their measurements of the classroom in a chart then organize their discoveries from the unit to make a Learning Scroll.

Appendices 68

Unit Overview

$\mathbb{T}$he focus of this unit is the further development of children's ideas about linear measurement. A previous CFLM unit, *Farms and Fences*, provided children multiple opportunities to measure with non-standard units and to develop an understanding of the need for standard units of measure. In that unit, children were introduced to the foot and the centimeter. *Tanisha and Tamika's Toolbox* builds on that understanding and introduces several new measuring tools: the tape measure, the yardstick, the inch, and the meter stick. Children are asked to select and use an appropriate tool, to compare and relate the tools, to construct the need for decomposition of units into smaller units, to use addition and subtraction to determine lengths, and to represent sums and differences on a number line diagram. 

The unit makes use of the double number line to support a strong sense of equivalence and to provide a potential challenge to those interested in exploring ways to convert from one measure to another. It is designed to align with the CCSS Standards of Mathematical Practice and the following core objectives:

Measurements & Data 2.MD: Measure and estimate lengths in standard units.

CCSS.Math.Content.2.MD.A.1

Measure the length of an object by selecting and using appropriate tools such as rulers, yardsticks, meter sticks, and measuring tapes.

CCSS.Math.Content.2.MD.A.2

Measure the length of an object twice, using length units of different lengths for the two measurements; describe how the two measurements relate to the size of the unit chosen.

CCSS.Math.Content.2.MD.A.3

Estimate lengths using units of inches, feet, centimeters, and meters.

CCSS.Math.Content.2.MD.A.4

Measure to determine how much longer one object is than another, expressing the length difference in terms of a standard length unit.

Measurements & Data 2.MD: Relate addition and subtraction to length.

CCSS.Math.Content.2.MD.B.5

Use addition and subtraction within 100 to solve word problems involving lengths that are given in the same units, e.g., by using drawings (such as drawings of rulers) and equations with a symbol for the unknown number to represent the problem.

CCSS.Math.Content.2.MD.B.6

Represent whole numbers as lengths from 0 on a number line diagram with equally spaced points corresponding to the numbers 0, 1, 2, …, and represent whole-number sums and differences within 100 on a number line diagram.

The Landscape of Learning

BIG IDEAS
❖ Lengths can be compared as repetitions (iterations) of shorter units
❖ Smaller units produce a greater value than larger units
❖ A standard unit allows people to get the same measurement
❖ Larger units can encompass (and be decomposed into) smaller units
❖ Unitizing
❖ Part/whole integration: lengths can be added and subtracted
❖ Conservation of length: equivalence
❖ Equivalent measurements can be exchanged
STRATEGIES
❖ Uses standard units and counts
❖ Uses standard units and estimates
❖ Decomposes unit into smaller units using estimation
❖ Decomposes unit into smaller units using halving
❖ Decomposes unit into smaller units using division
❖ Chooses appropriate units in relation to objects being measured
❖ Uses addition to determine overall length
❖ Counts on
❖ Uses subtraction to determine the length of a missing piece
❖ Decomposes and switches units when needed
MODELS
❖ Tape measure / measuring stick
❖ Number Line
❖ Double Number Line

The Mathematical Landscape

Tanisha and Tamika's Toolbox is designed to support the development of linear measurement. Current research (Sarama et. al. 2011) describes this development along a learning trajectory comprised of a series of levels with associated action schemes: (1) pre-length quantity recognizer (does not identify length as an attribute); (2a) length quantity recognizer (compares objects directly by lining them up next to each other); (2b) compares objects indirectly using a third object (transitivity); (3) point-to-point length measurer (may use a tower of cubes, but may not recognize the need to use the same size units and may leave gaps between units); (4) length unit relater and repeater (iterates a single unit back-to-back without gaps and knows the size of the unit matters); (5) length measurer (measures knowing the need for identical units, knows the relationship between units, partitions units, and adds to get accumulated distances). Piaget and Inhelder (1967) have also researched and written extensively on the development of the quantification and conservation of length. Conservation of length is usually constructed around the ages of 8 or 9.

By second grade most children have become length unit relaters and repeaters (level 4). They iterate a single unit back-to-back without gaps and they know the size of the unit matters, but they often know little about the available standard units of measure and when they might be helpful. They also may have little understanding of decomposition and the relationship of inches to feet and feet to yards, or centimeters to meters, and they most likely do not yet conserve length.

The investigations in this unit support children to move from level 4 to level 5. They involve children in constructing and choosing appropriate tools and experiencing the need to decompose units for more exact measurement. They construct addition and subtraction strategies to determine overall length and explore relationships between some new tools: the tape measure, the yardstick, and the meter stick. As they continue with explorations in the unit, they are asked to explore when these tools might be helpful when they need to choose appropriate tools by analyzing the tasks at hand.

Although early measurement can generally be viewed as a progressive development through five levels, in reality, the movement from level to level is far more complex and non-linear. To become a competent measurer of length (level 5), a complex network of relations is needed comprised of big ideas, strategies, and models as shown on the Landscape of Learning on page 11. A description of each follows.

BIG IDEAS

As young children explore the investigations within this unit, several big ideas will likely arise. These include:

- ❖ *Lengths can be compared as repetitions (iterations) of shorter units*
- ❖ *Smaller units produce a greater value than larger units*
- ❖ *A standard unit allows people to get the same measurement*
- ❖ *Larger units can encompass (and be decomposed into) smaller units*
- ❖ *Unitizing*
- ❖ *Part/whole integration: lengths can be added and subtracted*
- ❖ *Conservation of length: equivalence*
- ❖ *Equivalent measurements can be exchanged*

❖ *Lengths can be compared as repetitions (iterations) of shorter units*

As their understanding of measurement deepens, children come to realize that length can be measured as a repetition (iteration) of shorter lengths within the whole. No longer are they just counting objects placed on a line; they are marking the line as smaller lengths within the larger span.

❖ *Smaller units produce a greater value than larger units*

At first children do not see the need for a standard unit, but as they mark lengths they construct the idea that when longer units are used the overall measurement will be a smaller number and, reciprocally, when shorter units are used the overall measurement will be a greater number. *Giant Steps* (sometimes called *Mother May I?*) is a traditional childhood game that provides opportunities for children to construct this idea. In this game children quickly come to realize that if they take five giant steps they will be much closer to the finish line than if they take five baby steps.

❖ *A standard unit allows different people to get the same measurement*

Children need many experiences measuring with different size units to construct the idea that if two people measure with different units, two different measurements will result. *Farms and Fences* is a series of investigations designed to support children over time to come to this realization and to then request a standard unit because they now see a need for it. At this point, the ruler and/or tape measure can be introduced with meaning. It is assumed that most children working with *Tanisha and Tamika's Toolbox* understand the need for a standard unit of measure. If this is not the case with your students, you might want to use the CFLM unit *Farms and Fences* first.

❖ *Larger units can encompass (and be decomposed into) smaller units*

Iterated smaller units (like inches) can be grouped into larger units (like feet), which in turn can be grouped into yards. As children come to realize that if larger units are used, less would be needed, they can more appropriately choose a unit to use to measure a given object. A 10-foot line might be better measured with a foot-long ruler than with inches, whereas a line less than a foot long might be best measured in inches. On the other hand, a larger unit may need to be decomposed for exactness. For example, measuring a 10-foot line with a yardstick would require decomposing the last yard into feet.

❖ *Unitizing*

With number, unitizing a group of 10 objects into 1 ten is a big idea. It requires multiplicative thinking as children grapple to understand 132, not just as 100 + 30 + 2, but as 13 tens, plus 2, and later as 13.2 tens. The case is no different with measurement units. As children compose and decompose units, they come to understand that a kilometer can simultaneously be seen as 1,000 meters, or as 100,000 centimeters. A yard can be seen as 3 feet, or as 36 inches.

❖ *Part/whole integration: lengths can be added and subtracted*

It is the integration of the smaller units with the whole into a part/whole structure that supports children to come to realize that lengths can be added and subtracted. Now they can add on and use several addition and subtraction strategies they may have developed in other CFLM number and operation units. For example, now they can defend why a length of 9 units when placed next to a length of 6 units will span a total length of 15 units. They no longer need to start at the zero point and count every unit by ones. They count on from 9 or they understand how 9 + 6 can be interchanged with 10 + 5 because they are equivalent expressions.

❖ *Conservation of length: equivalence*

At first children may think that the length of a zigzagged fence may be shorter than the same length when straightened. They may argue that a fence on two sides of a rectangular shape (length plus width) is not the same length as when that section of fence is straightened out into one line. They will need many opportunities to measure and transform the segments of fencing into one straight line to construct this idea. Eventually an understanding that the length is conserved will develop and children will be able to explore and defend how lengths can be equivalent even when they are not straight lines, look different from each other, and are comprised of different smaller lengths.

❖ *Equivalent measurements can be exchanged*

Once children construct conservation of length and unitizing and have had ample opportunities to work with a variety of measurement units, they begin to understand that various units can be used to describe length and distance, and that equivalent pieces can be exchanged.

STRATEGIES

As you work with the activities in this unit, you will notice that students will use many strategies to solve the problems that are posed to them. Here are some strategies to notice:

- ❖ *Uses standard units and counts*
- ❖ *Uses standard units and estimates*
- ❖ *Decomposes units into smaller units using estimation*
- ❖ *Decomposes units into smaller units using halving*
- ❖ *Decomposes units into smaller units using division*
- ❖ *Chooses appropriate units in relation to objects being measured*
- ❖ *Counts on*
- ❖ *Uses addition to determine overall length*
- ❖ *Uses subtraction to determine the length of a missing piece*
- ❖ *Decomposes and switches units when needed*

❖ *Uses standard units and counts*

Once children construct the idea that the size of the unit used matters, they come to the realization that a standard unit is necessary for reliable measurement comparisons. They use a ruler and mark carefully the endpoints. Sometimes however, children have been told to use a ruler before fully developing an understanding of the many precursor strategies and big ideas described above. Thus, they use the tool but leave gaps and see no need to use the ruler carefully as an iterated unit. They don't fully comprehend its purpose.

❖ *Uses standard units and estimates*

When children first start using measurement tools, they treat the unit as a whole and measure end to end. When they discover the tool is too short, they report that the length is a little bit more, or a little bit less. They estimate rather than determining an exact measure. For example, when measuring a length of 14 inches with a ruler, they report that it is a little bit longer than a foot.

❖ *Decomposes unit into smaller units using estimation*

Precisely because most contexts demand exact measurements (building a box with only approximate measurements would likely result in a rather unstable, uneven box!), measurement units, to be useful, need to be decomposed into smaller units. When trying to decompose a foot into smaller equal parts, children will often begin by using perception alone. They estimate where some smaller marks might go, often erasing several times trying to adjust to make the intervals equal, eventually becoming satisfied with their adjustments.

❖ *Decomposes unit into smaller units using halving*

Decomposing by estimating and adjusting, however, is not sustainable. The need for exactness when measuring is important, and children tire of drawing and erasing. They seek out other strategies. In this unit, we provide children with foot-long paper strips, a medium that supports the evolution of some further strategies. Children usually halve, then halve again to make fourths, and then halve again to make eighths. This will be a nice strategy eventually to understand the fractional inch markers on a ruler, but making eighths of a foot is not very helpful for finding 12 inches as the eighth is 1.5 inches. This creates a new dilemma as children grapple to find 12 equal inches on their strips. Breaking the 3 inches up into 3 equal pieces by folding is difficult. Be prepared to see some children wanting to trim their foot-long piece when their folding does not result in 3 equal pieces! This is a nice moment to revisit measurement. You might ask, "Would the foot-long piece still measure exactly one foot, or would the whole measurement now be off?"

❖ *Decomposes units into smaller units using division*

As children decompose units they eventually construct the idea that they are dividing the unit into equal parts. This is a nice place to introduce fraction notation naturally: one foot divided into two equal parts is ½; thus 6 inches is ½ of a foot. One inch is 1/12 of a foot. The bar in fraction notation indicates division.

❖ *Chooses appropriate units in relation to objects being measured*

Once children have built several tools from decomposing and composing strategies, they are usually aware that certain tools have limitations and assets. They no longer just choose a tool and estimate the leftover; they know different tools allow for exactness when needed and they choose an appropriate tool to work with depending on the task.

❖ *Counts on*

Earlier in development, children just counted the number of feet by ones and marked them. Now they count on; for example, they may mark 4 feet, then count on 4 inches. At first they may forget the units they are working with and say, "5, 6, 7, 8." If so, stay grounded in the context as you confer and question, supporting them to realize that they do not have 8 feet. They have marked out 4 feet and 4 inches. They may also count on appropriately, for example if one side of a box (for example, the length) measures 9 feet and the other (width) measures 3 feet, they will count on from 9 ft., saying, " 10, 11, 12 ft."

❖ *Uses addition to determine overall length*

If one section measures 9 feet and the other measures 3 feet, rather than counting all of the units children add the measurements saying, "9 feet + 3 feet = 12 feet"

❖ *Uses subtraction to determine the length of a missing piece*

Subtraction is used to calculate the measurement of missing pieces. For example, if a total length is known, as well as a given piece, subtraction is used to determine the length of the missing unknown section. Or, when comparing two lengths, students subtract to find the difference.

❖ *Decomposes and switches units when needed*

Once children construct the big idea that equivalent lengths can be exchanged, a multitude of possible conversions results. Something that measures 4 inches plus 6 inches is equivalent to something that measures 3 inches plus 7 inches. But also, something that measures 1 foot and 6 inches can be thought of as 18 inches, or as ½ of a yard. With the metric system, something that measures a meter plus 50 cm can be thought of as 150 cm, 15 decimeters, or as 1 ½ meters. Some children may even become intrigued with the relationship between a centimeter and an inch. The conversion rate of 2.54 centimeters = 1 inch is quite close to 2 ½ cm for every inch, and you may find some of your children saying 5 cm is the same as 2 inches, so 10 cm must be 4 inches, etc. Although this is not an exact conversion, encourage it, as it is an early form of proportional reasoning! As they continue up the scale they will begin to see that their conversion is becoming increasingly off a bit. This is a nice opportunity to explore how their initial estimate of 2.5 must be a hair off, and now you can encourage them to ponder whether their estimate was a little under or a little over!

MATHEMATICAL MODELING

Model of a situation

Initially models emerge as a representation *of* a situation; later they are used by teachers to represent children's computation strategies. Ultimately they are appropriated by children as powerful tools *for* thinking (Gravemeijer, 1999). In this unit children measure using a ruler, yardstick, and meter stick, and construct their own tape measure. They use paper strips and eventually open number lines to represent the composition and decomposition of units. The double open number line model is introduced as a representation of the tools to explore grouping and unitizing, addition and subtraction, and equivalence and substitution.

The open number line encourages a linear representation of numbers and number operations for children that is powerful for developing mental arithmetic strategies (Beishuizen 1993; Klein, Beishuizen, and Treffers 2002). In this unit, the measurement tools show both the unit and the grouping (a foot as 12 inches, and 3 feet and 36 inches as a yard). The meter stick shows the centimeters and decimeters, as well as the inches (usually on the other side of the stick), to support grouping, equivalence, and the algebraic strategy of substituting an equivalent expression. Ultimately, these models will support students in converting from one unit to another effectively.

Model of Student Strategies

Children benefit from seeing the teacher model their strategies on an open number line. Once the model has been introduced as a representation of the situation, you can use it to model the children's strategies as they engage in minilessons on addition and subtraction. Notes are provided within the unit to help you do this, but if your school has purchased P2S2: a Personalized Professional Support System™ from New Perspectives Online (www.NewPerspectivesOnline.net), you will find it very helpful to go to *Digging Deep: Minilessons and Representations* to modules where Cathy explains in depth how to do this and where you can see videos of teachers doing minilessons with their children.

Model as a Tool for Thinking

Eventually children will be able to use the open number line as a tool for thinking about measurement. They will be able to imagine number as measurements on a number line and mentally mark lengths (and jumps) in various configurations. They will understand how equivalent length sections can be exchanged and the strategy of exchanging equivalent sections will support the development of fluency with addition and subtraction within 100. They will also have become skilled length measurers: measuring competently, knowing the need for identical units and the relationship between units, knowing how to partition units into smaller equal parts, and how to add, subtract, and exchange units to produce accumulated distances.

A graphic of the full landscape of learning for this unit is provided on page 11. The purpose of the graphic is to allow you to see the longer journey of students' measurement development and to place your work with this unit within the scope of this long-term development. You may also find the graphic helpful as a way to record the progress of individual students for yourself. Each landmark can be shaded in as you find evidence in a student's work and in what the student says—evidence that a landmark strategy, big idea, or way of modeling has been constructed. Or, you may prefer to use our web-based app (www.NewPerspectivesOnAssessment.com) to document your children's growth digitally. In a very real sense, you will be recording the individual pathways your students take as they develop as young mathematicians.

References and Resources

Beishuizen, Meindert (1993). Mental strategies and materials or models for addition and subtraction up to 100 in Dutch second grades. *Journal for Research in Mathematics Education, 24,* 294–323.

Gravemeijer, Koeno (1999). How emergent models may foster the constitution of formal mathematics. *Mathematical Thinking and Learning 1* (2): 155–77.

Klein, Anton S., Meindert Beishuizen, and Adri Treffers (2002). The empty number line in Dutch second grade, In *Lessons learned from research,* eds. Judith Sowder and Bonnie Schapelle. Reston, VA: NCTM.

Piaget, Jean and Barbel Inhelder (1967). The child's conception of space. New York: Norton.

Spelke, Elizabeth, Sang Ah Lee, and Veronique Izard (2010). Beyond core knowledge: natural geometry. *Cognitive Science.* May 1: 34 (5): 863-884.

Sarama, Julie and Douglas Clements, Jeffrey Barrett, Douglas W. Van Dine, Jennifer S. McDonel (2011). Evaluation of a learning trajectory for length in the early years. *Mathematics Education.* 43: 667-680.

SYSTEMS OF MEASUREMENT

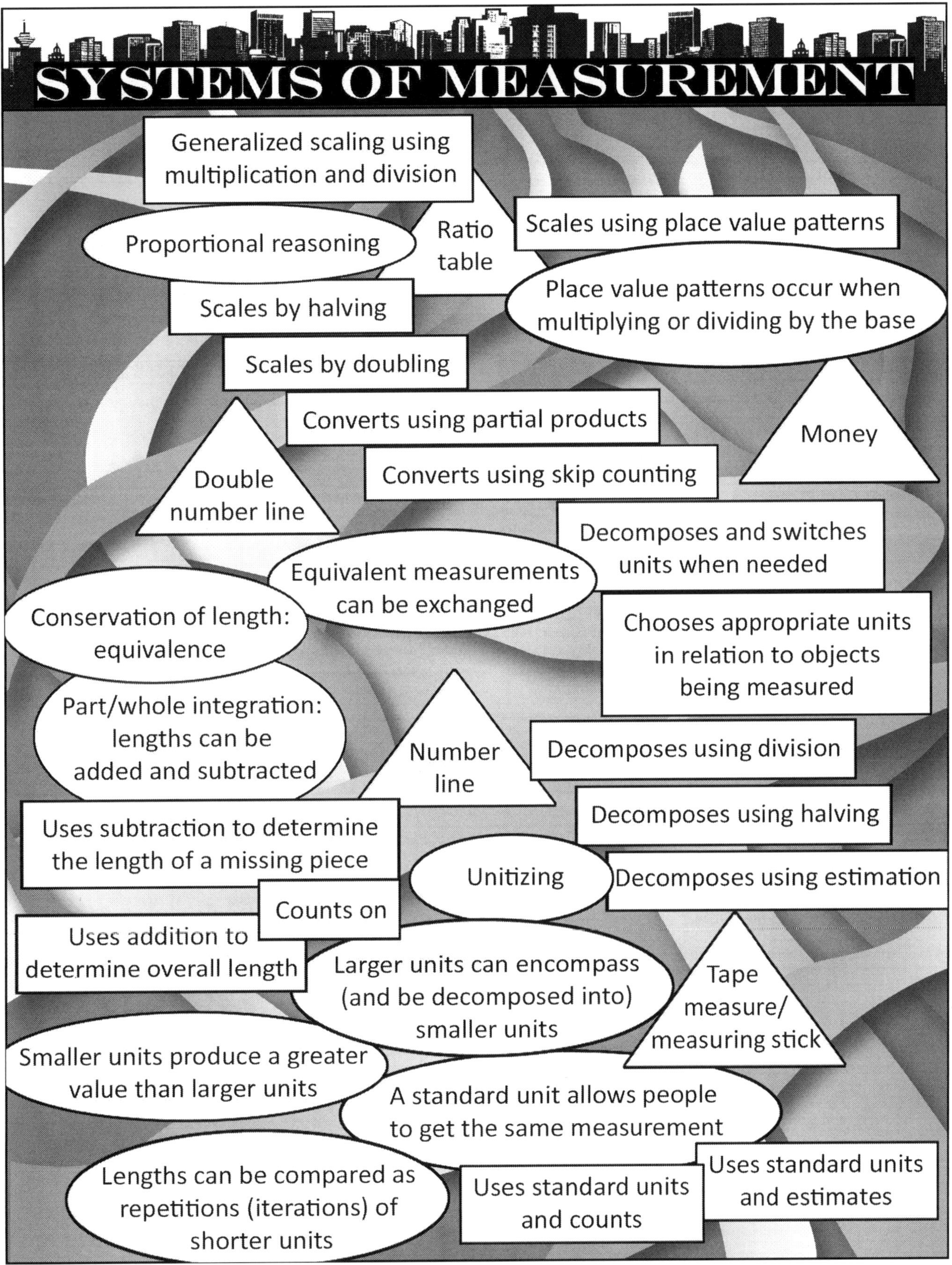

The landscape of learning: systems of measurement on the horizon showing landmark strategies (rectangles), big ideas (ovals), and models (triangles).

THE STANLEY FATMAX 25

Materials Needed

One yardstick and one ruler per pair of students

One roll of adding machine paper per pair of students

Tanisha and Tamika's Toolbox, Part One (Appendix A)

The Stanley FatMax 25 (Appendix B, 1 per pair of students)

Pencils, markers, scissors, and tape

Several sheets of copy or drawing paper

Blank Chart Paper for posters

This unit begins by introducing (or re-introducing) Tamika, from *Measuring for the Art Show*, and her friend Tanisha. If your students have previously worked through *Measuring for the Art Show*, they will likely remember how Tamika and her classmates helped their teacher build a measuring strip and blueprint for signs for an art show. It is not necessary to have done this earlier unit first. That unit used non-standard units and its purpose was to generate the open number line model. The purpose of this unit is the development of linear measurement systems. It is intended to follow *Farms and Fences*, the CFLM unit that introduces the standard foot. *Tanisha and Tamika's Toolbox* begins with Tanisha's curiosity about her dad's measuring tape. It is a professional carpenter's tape measure that is 25 feet long and the girls set off to see how long that is. On Day One, your students will engage in the same investigation, using a roll of adding machine paper and some tools: a ruler and a yardstick.

Day One Outline

Developing the Context

❖ Read the first part of the story *Tanisha and Tamika's Toolbox*, Appendix A, stopping at the place marked.

❖ Have students predict how long they think 25 feet will be.

❖ Send students off in pairs to measure out a 25-foot strip of paper, determining the length of the line in yards and inches.

Supporting the Investigation

❖ Confer with children as they work, noting the strategies they use and how they convert between units.

❖ Support students to note that as the units of measure increase in size, the amount of units needed decreases and the arithmetic becomes easier. Encourage them to explain why. As students finish, ask them to prepare a poster to convince others of their solutions and important things they have noticed. These posters will be used on Day Two in a gallery walk and math congress.

Developing the Context

Read Tanisha and Tamika's Toolbox, Appendix A, stopping at the place marked. After developing the story, display Appendix B. Explain that the task is to measure out a 25-foot long strip of paper from the roll students are given to see how long 25 feet is. Provide students with two tools: a ruler and a yardstick. Don't explain that a yard has 3 feet! Let children discover that as they work.

Assign math partners and send students off to measure. You may want to allow some groups to work in the hallway or another large space so that they can unroll the paper as they work. Provide drawing paper and pencils in case students wish to draw a line to model the problem as they do the arithmetic.

Tech Tip

To develop the context, many teachers take a photo of Appendix A with a cell phone or iPad and project it. Others use a document camera to project the page onto a whiteboard or screen.

Supporting the Investigation

As students begin to work, note with a quick look around if all students are engaged and understand the context. Work first to ensure students understand the context and then sit and confer with a few pairs as they work.

Some students may start with the ruler and mark the end, laying the next iteration next to the end of the first and marking again. Note if they leave gaps or if they overlap marks. How do they mark the 12 inches? Do they realize that 1 foot is simultaneously 12 inches? How do they determine the total number of inches? If some complain that they don't know how to do the inches, you might remind them that mathematicians often start by trying to model the problem. A model has been subtly introduced on the page—the double number line. Suggest that students draw what they know on the line. The double number line can be used to show inches, feet, and yards simultaneously. Encourage the modeling because this will help children see what can be exchanged. Each jump of 3 feet represents a yard, so there are 8 yards and 1 foot in 25 feet.

Some children might try to skip count by twelves to find the total number of inches. As you confer, suggest that they might try regrouping some of the groups to make the adding easier. For example they could break up the 12 into 10 and 2. Now they have 25 tens (which they can probably solve by skip counting by tens and keeping track); and they have 25 twos (which they can probably solve by skip counting by twos). This is a beautiful precursor strategy for the use of partial products as students move into multiplication in the future. Other students may regroup by adding 12 + 12 and getting groups of 24 or, encouraged by use of the yardstick they may make groups of 36. Encourage these students to see that the three groups of 12 are simultaneously three feet and that all together the groups of 36 inches that they have now are each equal to one yard.

Heather (the teacher): I've been watching what you two are doing and it looks like such an interesting strategy. Can I sit and confer with you?

Cole and Kashia: Sure! We are measuring with the ruler and making marks at the end.

Heather: That is what interested me. Do you know how long the ruler is? How will you know when you have made a long strip of 25 feet?

Kashia: Oh yeah! *(She takes a look at the ruler.)* It's 12 inches. We should write "12" every time!

Heather: Hmm…that's interesting, isn't it? So each time you lay down the ruler it's 12 inches. But what does that tell us about the 25 feet?

Kashia: Um…

Cole: I thought it was a foot already.

Heather: You're right, this ruler is 1 foot long. So this ruler is showing us 1 foot and 12 inches at the same time. That's efficient!

Cole: Yep, so the next mark is 2… feet, and another 12 inches. *(They continue on in this fashion. They have marked out 6 feet when Heather decides it's time for a challenge.)*

Heather: So you have marked out 6 feet so far and you still have a long way to go to get to 25 feet. This is going to be a lot of work, isn't it? And then you are going to have to add up all of the inches, too. Have you considered using the yardstick? Do you think that would help? How does it compare to the foot?

Kashia: It's longer. *(She measures the yardstick with the ruler.)* It is 3 feet long and it says 36" on it.

Cole: I think we should use that. We wouldn't have as many marks to make. *(He lays it down on the strip and notices that his 3 marks—and the 3 twelves—line up with the end of the yardstick.)* Now we don't even have to add 12 and 12 and 12. It's 36 inches. We can mark that, too!

Heather: Do you want to check?

Cole: 10, 20, 30, ….and 2, 4, 6….so that's 36. See, I was right!

Author's notes

Heather notes that the pair is measuring with the ruler, marking each time at the end. She sits down and starts the conferral by getting clarification on whether they know how long the ruler is. This question forces them to examine the meaning of the numbers on the ruler and in the problem.

Heather focuses on the equivalence and celebrates that Cole is marking both inches and feet.

Introducing the yardstick for consideration provides a nice challenge. Students are now considering the big idea that the longer the tool, the fewer iterations needed.

Once again, equivalence is a central idea. 36 inches equals 1 yard equals 3 feet.

Heather: Wow! So now you are doing feet and inches and yards all at the same time! This is a great strategy! Do you think if you kept working with the yardstick, you could measure 25 feet? **Cole:** Yep. Let's do it, Kashia. This is a good strategy! The yardstick is easier. **Heather:** What's making it easier? **Cole:** It's longer. We are doing 3 feet at a time! **Heather:** This strategy will be important to share when you make your poster later. With the yardstick you were doing 3 feet at a time!	*These are big ideas for these young mathematicians and Heather celebrates their strategy with them again.*

As students begin to reach conclusions about how long the FATMAX 25 is in inches and yards, ask them to prepare posters presenting their findings for a gallery walk and congress on Day Two. Explain that mathematicians often want to share their findings with each other, and that when they do they are careful to choose the most important ideas to share. As students prepare their work on poster paper, they should not copy or explain every step they took. Instead, encourage students to record how their thinking changed, the interesting connections they noticed, and the arguments they used to convince each other that their answers were correct. How did they find the inches and yards? Did they do the inches first, and then the yards, or the reverse? Did they convert? Why? What did they notice along the way that might have made their work easier?

Teacher Note: Number Lines

An open number line can be a powerful tool to represent equivalent measurements. Encourage your students to record their measurements on an open number line as they progress in their work or begin making posters to share their ideas. Have they reached 4 feet and 48 inches? Draw a line, mark it with a starting point, and suggest that students show that the 4 feet and 48 inches line up at the same spot. Where did the yard line up? Now they have another point on their number line and a new challenge. Where will the second yard take them? If they skip counted by 12 to find the number of inches, does recording their ideas on the number line suggest more efficient strategies, such as skip counting by 36? For more on the open number line, see the student work and dialogue box on Day Two.

Reflections on the Day

Today students were asked to measure length, and to convert between inches, yards, and feet. The double number line (which may have emerged as a representation of the measuring tape) can be used as a helpful tool in converting from one unit to another. Along the way students most likely came to realize that as the unit used became bigger, the number of times they needed to iterate it was proportionately smaller. Day Two's math congress will provide an opportunity for a rich discussion about ways to convert from one unit to another and how larger units reduce the number of iterations needed and can require far less work! On the other hand, when the distance is smaller than a yard (such as the last foot of the measuring tape) switching to a different unit of measure may be necessary.

HOW LONG IS 25 FEET?

Materials Needed

Students' work from Day One

Rulers and yardsticks

Pencils and markers

Sticky notes (about 3 per student)

Today begins with a minilesson as a warm-up to math workshop. Students work with a string of related problems designed to further support the conversion of one unit to another. After the minilesson, students put finishing touches on their posters and a gallery walk ensues to provide students with opportunities to read and write viable arguments—an important standard of mathematical practice. After the gallery walk a math congress is held to discuss a few of the pieces more deeply.

Day Two Outline

Minilesson: A String of Related Problems
❖ Work on a string of related problems designed to encourage students to convert fluently using multiplicative structuring.

Facilitating the Gallery Walk
❖ Confer with children as they put finishing touches to their posters, asking them to consider the most important things they want to tell their audience about smart ways to convert.
❖ Conduct a gallery walk to allow students time to reflect and comment on each other's posters from Day One.

Facilitating the Math Congress
❖ Convene students at the meeting area to discuss a few strategies students used to find the measurements.
❖ Examine how some strategies, such as those with smaller units, required a great deal of measuring and arithmetic, while others with larger units were more efficient.
Did some students convert units directly to check their measurements? This is a key moment to discuss equivalence!

Minilesson: A String of Related Problems

This string is designed to help students convert more flexibly from one unit to another. Represent the problems on a double number line like the one below, one problem at a time, and invite students to share their conversion strategies. As they do, draw their thinking on the open number line to show the equivalence. For example, if a student says "3 feet," draw three equal jumps underneath the line, inside the yard, showing them as equal to the yard. If a student says "36 inches," write it either at the top above 1 yard, or directly under it.

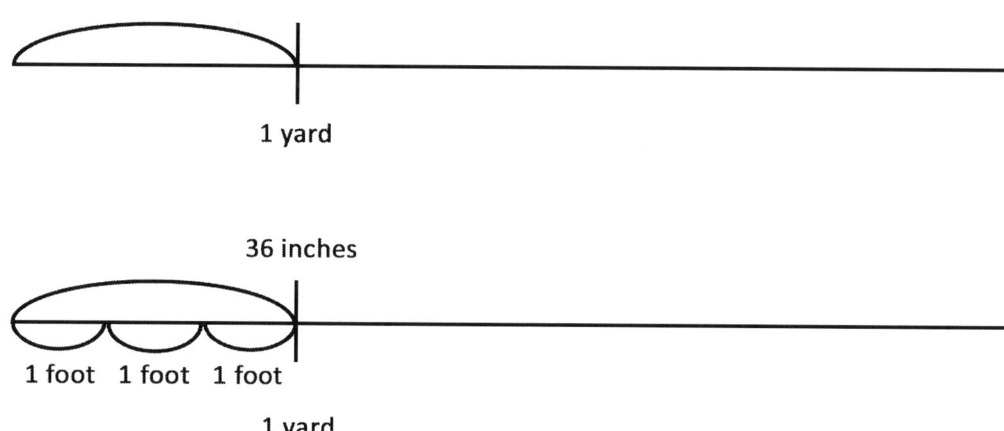

The String:

1 yard

9 feet

2 yards

4 yards

5 feet

Inches	Feet	Yards
		1
	9	
		2
		4
	5	

Teacher Note: Representing Multiplicative Strategies

Your class may have some students who are able to think about these problems multiplicatively, while others are still using additive structuring. As you progress through the problems, ground students in the number line representation. 9 feet is 9 groups of 12 inches and 4 yards is 4 groups of 3 feet. Make sure that all students can see these relationships on the number line to support them in understanding their peers' strategies.

Facilitating the Gallery Walk

Ask students to return to the posters they began on Day One, adding any finishing touches they desire. The posters should describe their strategies and the important things they noticed. If the 25-foot paper strip is important to their strategy, they can tape or pin it next to the poster. Move around and confer as students work, asking them to consider the most important things they want to tell their audience about smart ways to measure and convert. Remind them that it is not necessary to write about everything they did, but instead to concentrate on convincing their audience about the important things they discovered and want to defend. Depending on how much prior experience your students have had doing gallery walks, it may be helpful to provide instructions before you pass out the sticky notes. If your students have not done a gallery walk for some time, or if you think they need more instruction on how to proceed, see the Teacher Note section below.

Teacher Note

Let your students know that their comments and questions should be specific about the math on the poster, and to steer clear of comments such as "Good job!" or "I like your poster." Remind students that mathematicians write to convince other mathematicians that they are right. Thus, specific comments and questions are most helpful. It may help to give the example of writing workshop, since most students can remember a time when a peer said something like, "I like your story!" but did not explain why. Once you have gone over a few examples and perhaps even modeled writing a comment or question, pass out the sticky notes. Explain that you are going to start by passing out three sticky notes, and students can return to get more if needed.

Ask students to start at different places and choose three or four posters to focus on. Remind them to read carefully and then to leave a sticky note at several posters, enough so that after about ten minutes all posters will have at least a few comments. Remind students that gallery walks should be quiet times so that all reviewers can read and think before commenting. This time should be taken seriously. One of the Standards of Mathematical Practice is to read and write viable arguments and this is a time to foster the development of that ability.

After the gallery walk, invite the groups to go back to their posters to see what comments and questions were left. Allow a few minutes for everyone to think about the feedback they received and to discuss any new ideas with their partners before convening the whole class in the meeting area for a congress.

Facilitating the Congress

Review the posters and choose a few that you can use for a discussion that will deepen understanding and support growth along the landscape of learning described in the overview. There is not necessarily one best plan for a congress. There are many different plans that might all be supportive of development.

If your school has purchased P2S2™, the support system for CFLM (www.NewPerspectivesOnline.net), you will have access to many tips about how to plan congresses. For example, you might start with a sample pair of students that used the ruler to measure as shown in Figure 1. They may have tried to skip count by 12, tediously working to get a total of the number of inches first. Note whether they left gaps or overlapped a few of the feet and if so discuss with the class whether gaps matter. Starting the math congress with a piece like this will also serve as a support for other students who may have found skip counting or repeated addition difficult.

Figure 1. Students use the ruler to skip count the inches.

Look for a poster where 3 feet is circled and shown as 1 yard, as in Figure 2. This gives you a chance to foster discussion on the equivalence and to examine how using a bigger tool meant fewer steps. See if students can explain why that is and promote discussion on whether all the answers are equivalent:

300 inches = 25 feet = 8 yards plus 1 foot = 8 yards plus 12 inches

Figure 2. Each group of 3 feet is 1 yard.

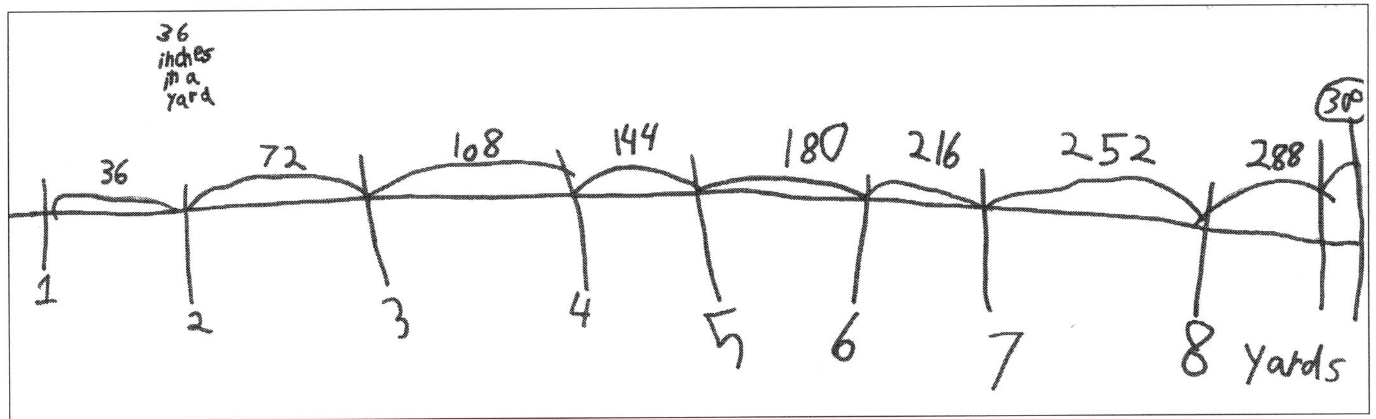

Figure 3. Each yard is 36 more inches.

Whatever pieces you decide to use, make sure that one of the big ideas discussed is that the longer the units used when measuring, the fewer the number of iterations. Using yards produces an answer of 8 (plus a foot), whereas using feet produces a length of 25, and using inches produces an answer of 300. Promote discussion on how all of these measurements are correct. Since a yard is 3 times as big as a foot, the number of yards is 3 times smaller than the total number of feet. Despite the different numbers, the measurements are equivalent.

Inside One Classroom: A Portion of the Math Congress

Several students have already presented, and Heather calls the group whose work is shown in figure 3 to conclude the congress.

Kevin: To find the inches, Hawa was counting out for each foot, but then it was so big that she forgot how many she had and didn't know when to stop.

Hawa: Yeah, it was too many. But Kevin only had 8 yards and a foot so we decided to use that to find the inches instead of going back.

Kevin: I used the number line. I've always used it since last year and it makes the problem simpler to keep track. So we put the yards on the bottom and the inches on the top and counted by 36s like Ryan and Eva. We got 288 for the 8 yards and 12 more for the foot, so it was 300 inches.

Heather: Wow, that number line does make it easier to keep track of the numbers, doesn't it? Does anyone see a connection between their work and what Kevin and Hawa did?

Amelia: We got the same numbers but we wrote them as adding. 36+36=72. 72+36=108 and we kept going like that.

Hawa: But how did you know when to stop?

Author's notes

Work with previous contexts and minilessons has helped Kevin internalize the single number line model as a tool for thinking about new problems. Note how he is able to build and share a double number line for this new context.

Ellie: The yards were 8 because 8 threes would be 24. So 8 yards and 1 more foot equals 25 feet. *(Most of the class seems confused by this statement.)*

Heather: Ellie, you were using the number of feet in each yard to find the total yards? I'm going to try to draw what you're saying on a number line like Kevin used. So here's one yard, and that is also 36 inches and also 3 feet? *(Heather draws the first yard on a number line and then adds to it as shown below.)* So how far is the next yard?

Ellie: 6. That is 3 plus 3.

Heather: Ah, yes. Another 3 feet. And can somebody else tell me about the third yard?

Kashia: It's 9 feet. Oh, like in the beginning of class!

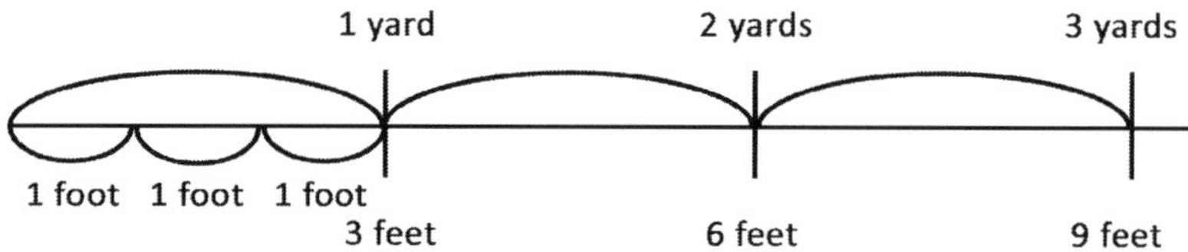

Heather: We did think about this in the beginning of class, didn't we? We could figure out the number of yards from the feet and the number of feet from the yards. What about 4 yards?

Cole: 11. No, wait… 9+3=12. 12.

(Heather continues calling on students to skip-count until the class reaches 8 yards/24 feet.)

Heather: So now we are at 8 yards and 24 feet, but we're not quite to 25. How much farther do we need to go?

Amelia: 12 inches!

Toby: 1 foot!

Amelia: Well, those are the same. 12 inches is the last foot.

Heather: I think either one of those would work. So 25 feet is equal to 8 yards and 1 foot, or 8 yards and 12 inches?

Kevin: And 300 inches.

Heather is facilitating a very important shift here. As students marked their measurements on the paper strip, they were creating number lines as a model of their thinking. Now, however, Heather is encouraging them to adapt the number line as a tool for thinking about the number relationships.

Reflections on the Day

Math workshop began today with a minilesson that supported students in converting lengths within a linear system by making use of the relationships from a t-chart and representing them on a double number line to model the equivalence. The minilesson may have also helped your students refine their thinking as they prepared to share their posters. By participating in a gallery walk on their work from Day One, students had opportunities to read and write viable arguments and then consider their classmates' comments, questions, and suggestions. Opportunities like these are designed to support the development of proof-making. A math congress provided opportunities for further discussion and reflection on the topic of measurement conversion, and by the end of the day you may already be noticing how several of your students are starting to convert directly between equivalent measurements within a measurement system.

DAY THREE

TANISHA'S TOOL BELT

Today begins with a minilesson as a warm-up to math workshop. Students work with a string of related addition problems. After the minilesson a new context is presented. Tanisha has gotten a tool belt and in it is a shiny new tape measure. This tape measure is 60 inches long. Is it longer or shorter than her dad's FatMax 25? What is the difference between the two lengths?

Day Three Outline

Minilesson: A String of Related Problems
❖ Work on a string of related problems designed to encourage flexible mental math strategies for addition.

Developing the Context
❖ Using Appendix A, Part Two, tell the story of Tanisha's tool belt and the 60-inch tape measure.
❖ Distribute Appendix C and ask students to investigate which tape is longer and how much longer it is than the other.

Supporting the Investigation
❖ Confer with children as they work, noting the strategies they use and if and how they convert between different units.
❖ As students finish, ask them to prepare a poster to convince others of their solutions and important things they have noticed along the way. These posters will be used on Day Four in a gallery walk and congress.

Minilesson: A String of Related Problems

This mental math minilesson uses a string of related problems designed to encourage children to add by keeping one number whole and taking leaps of 10, then leaps for any remaining amount that needs to be added. Do one problem at a time and record children's strategies on an open number line, inviting other children to comment on the representations. As you progress through the string and notice children beginning to make use of the tens, discuss why this strategy is helpful. If the class agrees that it is a useful strategy for addition, you might want to make a sign for it and post it near the meeting area. Over time you will have several signs of "Helpful Addition and Subtraction Strategies" posted on a strategy wall. Name each strategy after the student mathematician who offers it.

The String:

138 + 10

138 + 20

138 + 23

138 + 19

367 + 34

367 + 29

Inside One Classroom: A Portion of the Minilesson

Heather (the teacher): Remember to show me with a "thumbs up" when you have had enough think time. Here's the first one: 138 + 10. *(Several thumbs go up quickly. This is an easy problem for the group.)* Frederick? You had that quickly and I saw that you didn't need to count. What did you do?

Frederick: 148. I knew there were 13 tens before, so one more made 14. *(Heather underlines the 13 in 138 and then the 14 in 148.)* Everyone, turn and talk to your elbow partner. How is Frederick thinking about the tens? Is he right, and how is it helping him? *(After a few minutes, Heather resumes whole class discussion.)*

Heather: So you turned and talked. Did anyone have an interesting or helpful partner?

Paulo: I did. I thought it was just 3 tens, but Kashia helped me understand that the hundred had 10 tens more. So it is 13 tens.

Heather: And so one more ten made it 14, so 148. Frederick has a nice way of thinking about the tens, doesn't he? Nice job at being a helpful partner, Kashia. Ok, let's go on. How about 138 + 20?

Author's notes

Heather encourages her students to think about the number of tens in 138, rather than the number of tens in the tens column. Doing so will build a nice foundation for division by ten, decimals and place value in later years. By fifth grade students should be able to consider 138 as 13.8 tens. Note the way Heather is developing community and respect among her students. She compliments them on being helpful partners and emphasizes that using someone's strategy is a compliment.

(Heather pauses for a moment of think time.)

Paulo: I used Frederick's strategy. Now it's 15 tens. So 158.

Heather: *(She underlines the 15.)* What a nice compliment for Frederick! Nice job, Paulo. Ok, how about 138 + 23?

Kallie: Now it is just 3 more. So 2 get me to 160, and 1 more is 161.

Heather draws an open number line and represents the earlier strategies and then Kallie's strategy as follows:

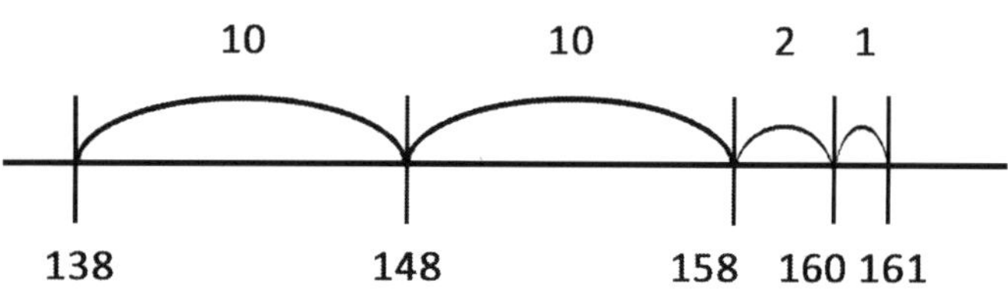

Heather: Wow, we're really getting good at this, aren't we? What about 138 +19?

Maia: I used the other problems. 138 + 20 = 158. 19 was 1 below 20, so I took away the 1. 157.

Eva: Oh yeah! I was counting up from 148, but that way is even better.

The representation of the addition on the open number line supports students to consider the magnitude of the numbers, how near they are, and how far they are from each other. Using a closed number line with a mark for each 1 encourages children to count. Instead, Heather supports leaps.

Developing the Context

Project a copy of Appendix A if you have the technology to do so, and read the next part of the story as you develop the context. If you don't have the technology, just read the story and show students the picture of Tanisha's tool belt. Remember to engage them in the story. Make the context come alive!

Pass out Appendix C and discuss the context to make sure students understand that one tape measure is 60 inches and the other is 25 feet. See which one they think is longer. Don't be surprised if some say, "60 is longer, because 60 is bigger than 25." Don't correct them at this point, just remind them that one is 60 inches and the other is 25 feet. Then send the students off in pairs to investigate. Point out that a number line has been drawn on Appendix C if they want to use it as a model. Don't tell them to label the mark on the left 60 and the 25 on the right. You will likely see some children put 25 on the left because the number is smaller. As you confer, this will provide for a rich conversation. Just remind students that the 25 is 25 feet and the 60 is 60 inches. You may find that the partners disagree, in which case you can support the student who realizes that the measurement units matter in justifying his or her reasoning to the partner. If both students feel that 25 feet is smaller, ask which measurement is longer, feet or inches. Suggest students look at a ruler and compare a foot with an inch if they are still puzzled. Finally, remind them that they have drawing paper, too, if they want to redraw the model to help them.

Supporting the Investigation

The line in Appendix C and the units given for each tape measure are chosen intentionally to push students to compare feet and inches. Be prepared that some students will label 25 on the left because "25 is a smaller number than 60." Here it is important to ask whether they think 25 feet is shorter or longer than 60 inches. If they aren't sure, suggest they work with the 60 inches and see how many feet it is. Some students may skipcount by 12 beginning with 1 foot, as in Figure 4, but other children may begin from a landmark like 36 inches = 3 feet (from the yardstick) or 48 inches = 4 feet (a common height at this age). A few students may remember from Day One that the 25 feet was 300 inches. If they work with inches, they will have to find the difference between 300 and 60. If they work with feet they will need to subtract: 25 – 5. Suggest that children try finding the difference both ways, exploring if the answers are equivalent. Of course, they will discover that 240 inches = 20 feet. Some students may even discover that the difference is also 6 yards and 2 feet.

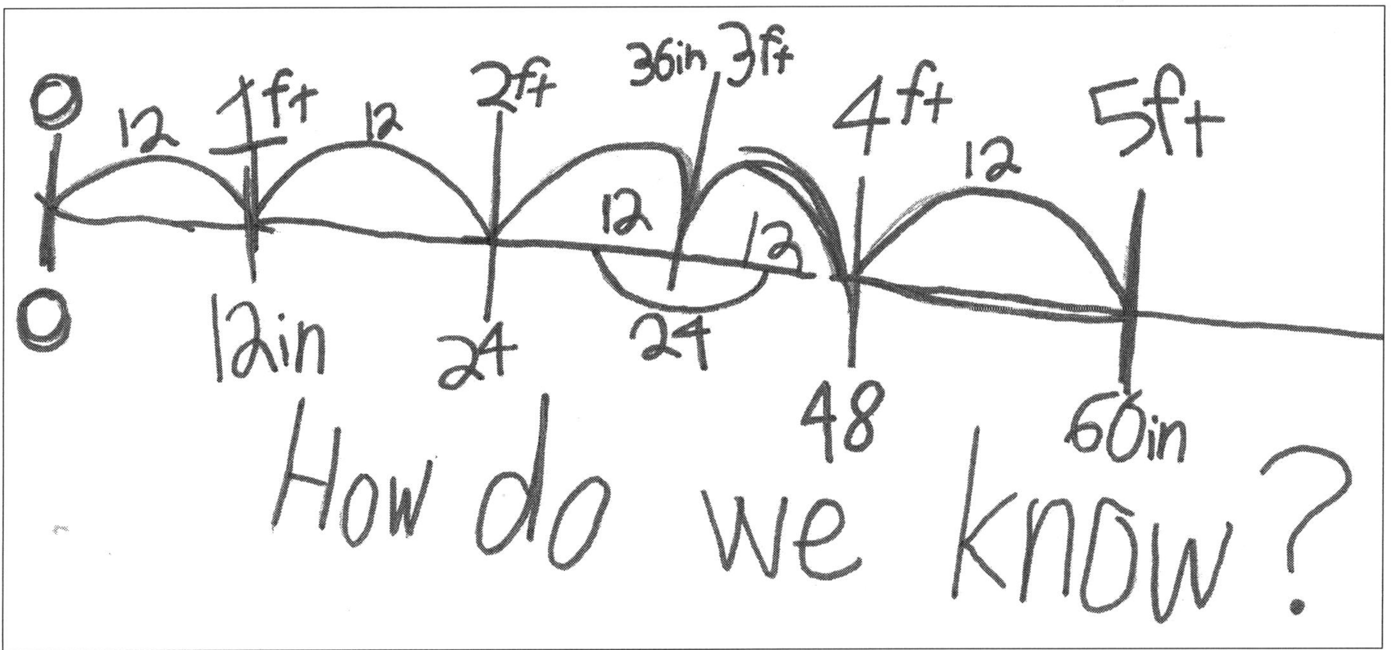

Figure 4. 60 inches = 5 feet

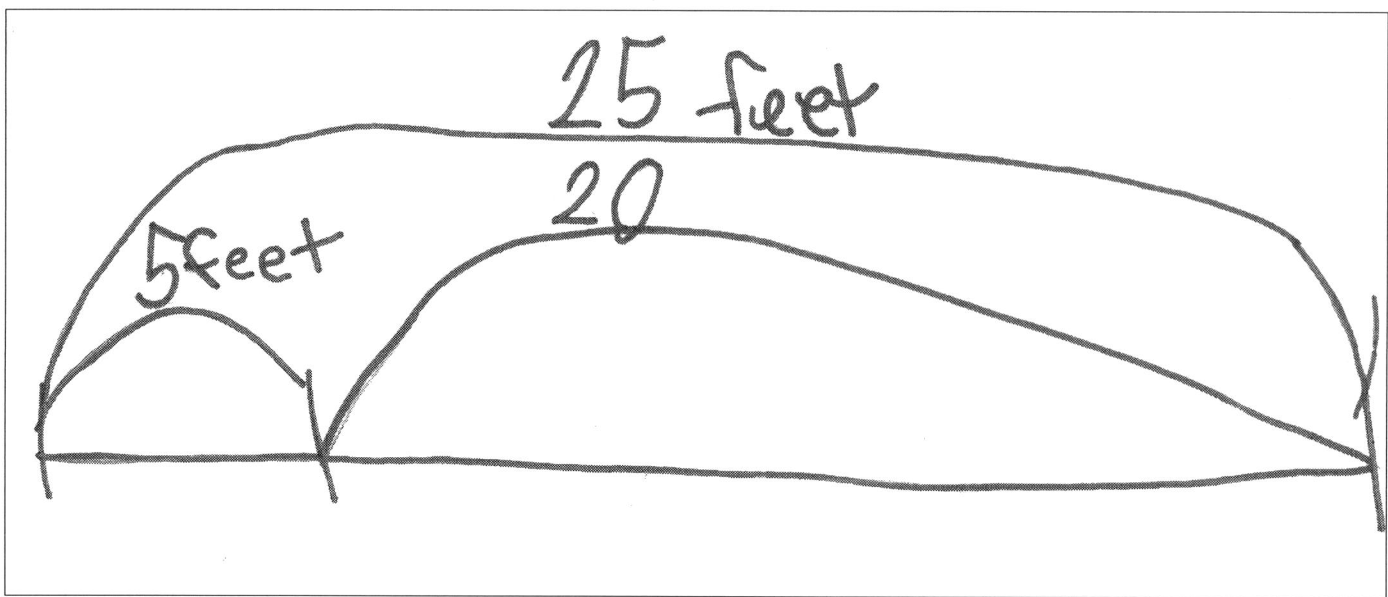

Figure 5. 25 feet = 5 feet + 20 feet

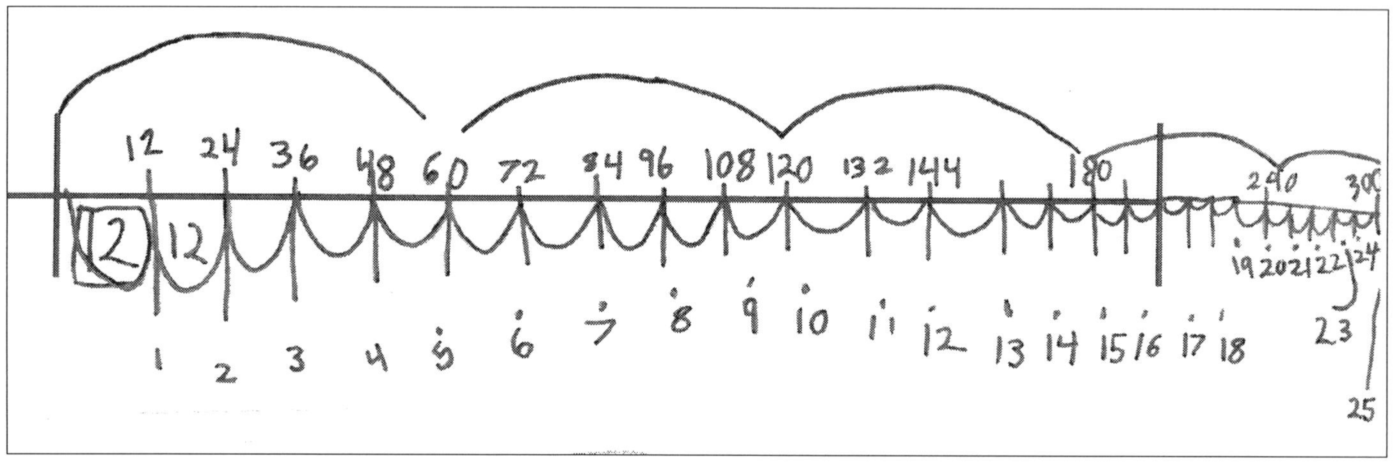

Figure 6. A student regroups 25 feet into 5 groups of 60 inches.

Children may select many different strategies to find the difference between the two lengths. Confer with children as they work, noting the strategies they use. Do they add on from 60 and go to 300 by adding 40 more first to get to a landmark 100? Or, do they remove 60 from 300? If they convert to feet first they can most likely do the arithmetic in their heads: $25 - 5 = 20$. This experience is invaluable in helping them to see the power of using an appropriate measurement tool and converting to simplify the arithmetic.

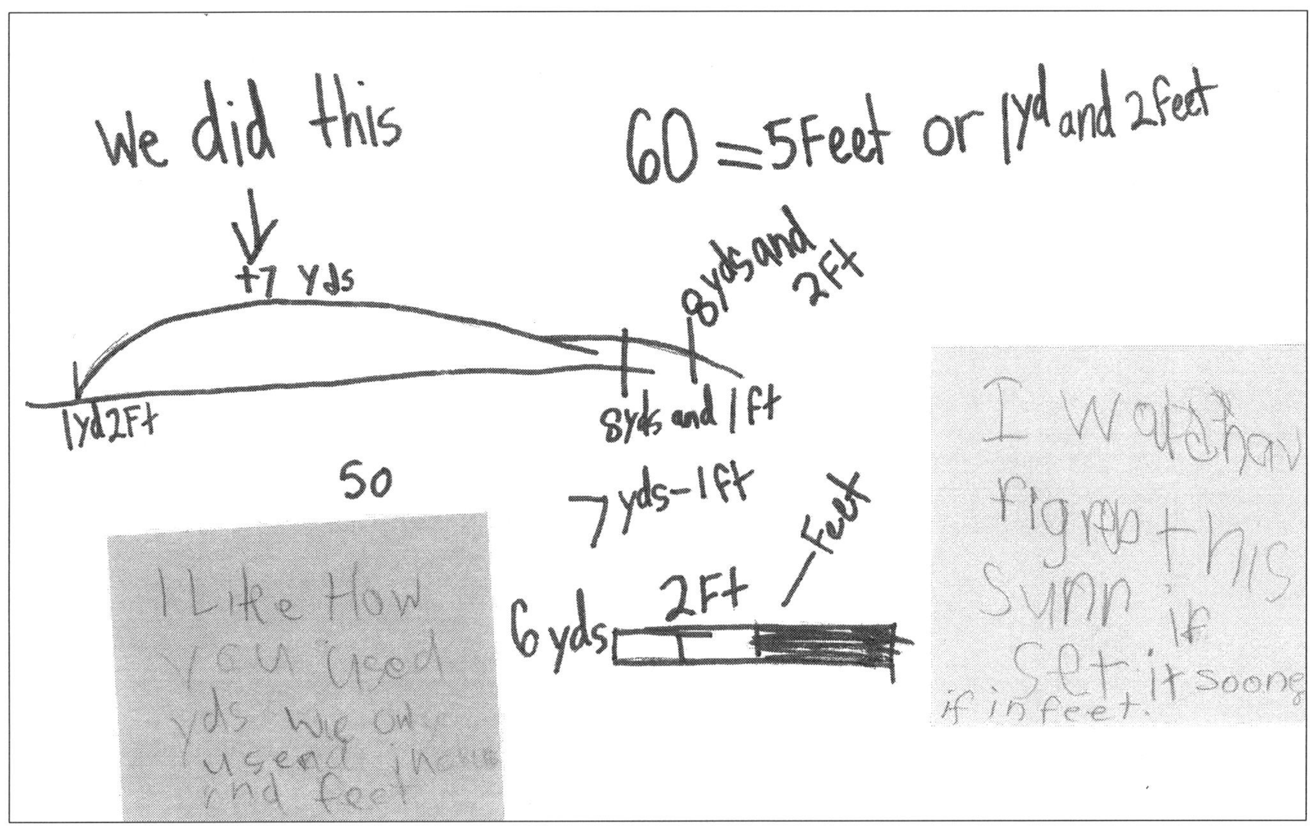

Figure 7. Students find the difference in yards: 6 yards and 2 feet.

Inside One Classroom: Conferring with Students at Work

Heather (the teacher): So I see that the two of you have started with a drawing. You have modeled the two lengths on an open number line. What a great idea! Models can be such powerful tools for mathematicians.

Sasha and Kashia: Yep. And we put 25 here and 60 over there and now we are making jumps from the 25 to get to the 60.

Heather: I see that. You chose a very helpful tool. Good choice! I have a question though. I'm curious. Why did you put 25 on the left and the 60 on the right?

Sasha: Because 25 comes first when you count. It is smaller than 60.

Heather: That's true. When you count, the number 25 does come before 60. But this 25 is 25 feet, and the 60 is 60 inches. Do you think that will matter? Which is longer, 1 foot or 1 inch? *(Heather has succeeded in creating disequilibrium. Both girls are now considering a big idea on the landscape: the bigger the length of the unit, the smaller the number of units needed.)*

Author's notes

Heather begins by celebrating how the pair has chosen a mathematical model, the number line, as a tool for thinking. Finding something to celebrate is a great way to start a conferral. Now she can challenge them without it feeling like a criticism.

Kashia: Oh…. The foot is longer. There's 12 inches in it! We need to make a new picture, Sasha. **Heather:** Do you remember from our congress yesterday how many inches were in the 25 feet? **Kashia:** 300? **Heather:** Yes, it was 300. So the FatMax 25 is 300 inches and Tanisha's tape measure is 60 inches. Which is longer? **Sasha:** The FatMax is a lot longer! **Heather:** And we are trying to figure out how much longer, right? It might be a good idea to change your picture….but your choice of the number line as a tool is a really good idea. How do you think you might change it? **Sasha:** We need to put 300 inches way out here *(pointing to the right side of the line)* and then see how many inches it is from 60 to 300. **Heather:** That sounds like a great plan. I'll check back with you later and you can let me know what you found out, ok?	*Reminding the girls of the work they had done yesterday helps them consider how many inches were in the 25 feet without having to do the work all over again. It also helps them reflect on the fact that 25 feet equal 300 inches. The longer the unit, the smaller the amount needed—a big idea on the landscape of learning.* *Heather has now succeeded in getting the girls to focus on the use of the model and to find the difference between 60 and 300. She leaves them so they have time to reflect independently on the new problem.*

It's likely that your students will be at many different places in their understanding. While some might be constructing the big idea that different units produce different number values, others may already be decomposing and switching units. The following dialogue box offers a glimpse at a very different conferral on the same task.

<table>
<tr><td colspan="2">Inside One Classroom: Conferring with Students at Work</td></tr>
<tr>
<td>

Heather (the teacher): So I see that the two of you have started with the inches on a number line. What a great idea! Models can be such powerful tools for mathematicians.

Eva and Kevin: Yep. We took two yards and that was 36 + 36, but we needed 30 + 30 so we took away the sixes.

Heather: That's a neat idea! So if you had 2 yards but then took away 6 inches twice, how much have you taken away?

Eva: 12 inches. Oh, so we took away a foot. So it's 6 feet minus 1.

</td>
<td>

Author's notes

Heather begins by celebrating how the pair has chosen a mathematical model, the number line, as a tool for thinking.

</td>
</tr>
</table>

Heather: Okay! Now we know that the little tape measure is 60 inches, and also 5 feet, and also 2 yards minus a foot. So how much bigger is the Fatmax?

Kevin: The Fatmax was 8 yards, so it's 6 yards longer.

Eva: 6 yards and 1 foot.

Heather: We could do it in yards, couldn't we? If the little one was 2 yards, we'd need 6 more plus 1 foot to reach 25 feet. But it was a little shorter than that. How long was it?

Eva: 5 feet. Oh yeah, that was 2 yards take away a foot.

Kevin: So it's 2 feet! We have to add that extra foot. So we jump 1 foot to 2 yards, then 6 yards, then another foot.

Eva: Yeah. It's 6 yards and 2 feet longer.

Heather: Wow, that was some impressing jumping on the number line. Good work! I hope you draw a really good number line on your poster so that everyone else can see this strategy that you used.

Eva and Kevin have internalized the yard as a useful unit—that's why they began with groups of 36 inches. Although the arithmetic is actually simpler with feet in this case, these students remember that yards simplified their work on earlier days. Heather sees from their use of the number line to decompose the yards and recompose a foot that they have a strong enough grounding to find the difference in yards.

As students finish, ask them to prepare a poster to convince others of their solutions and important things they have noticed along the way as they worked. These posters will be used on Day Four in a gallery walk and congress.

Reflections on the Day

Math workshop began today with a minilesson to support addition strategies. Then a new context was developed where children compared 60 inches to 25 feet. As you moved around and conferred you may have noticed that many students were converting more easily than on Day One. You are witnessing major development in front of your eyes and it is important to document it. Take a look at the landscape in the overview. Have you seen your children traversing the landscape? Document each child's journey. Some teachers make copies of the graphic of the landscape and use it to highlight each child's path as they grow and develop as mathematicians. There is also an app available if you wish to capture your students' development digitally. For information, go to www.NewPerspectivesOnAssessment.com.

DAY FOUR

WHICH MEASURING TAPE IS THE LONGEST?

Materials Needed

Pencils

Sticky notes

Drawing paper or several sheets of copy paper

Posters from Day Three and extra chart paper if needed (sticky note style is best as it makes taping on the walls unnecessary)

Markers

Today begins with students adding finishing touches to posters from Day Three and a gallery walk ensues. After the gallery walk a congress is held to discuss a few of the pieces more deeply. The congress ends with a minilesson. Students work with a string of related problems designed to support fluent converting from one unit to another.

Day Four Outline

Facilitating the Gallery Walk

❖ Confer with children as they put finishing touches to their posters, asking them to consider the most important things they want to tell their audience about smart ways to convert and smart ways to measure.

❖ Conduct a gallery walk to allow students time to reflect and comment on each other's posters.

Facilitating the Math Congress

❖ Convene students at the meeting area to discuss a few important ideas about converting from one unit of measure to another, and which way was the most efficient.

Minilesson: A String of Related Problems

❖ Work on a string of related problems designed to encourage efficient addition and subtraction.

Facilitating the Gallery Walk

Ask students to return to the posters they began on Day Three, adding any finishing touches they desire. As they work, move around and confer, asking them to consider the most important things they want to tell their audience about smart ways to convert. Remind them that it is not necessary to write about everything they did, but instead to concentrate on convincing their audience about the important things they discovered and want to defend.

The main purpose of a gallery walk is of course the development of the reading and writing of viable arguments, but a secondary purpose is to provide time for reflection, refinement, and consolidation of the thinking learners generated as they investigated the problem. Often when students are postering, the ideas they write about go beyond what they actually did. Students may have started with skip counting strategies or doing a great deal of arithmetic, but as they worked they might have had an insight on a more efficient strategy. They should focus their posters on the latter strategy, as that is an important insight to share. Encouraging students to just write about what they did may not be as supportive of development as encouraging them to write about an insight they had as they worked and to write a convincing argument about it. The former is more about narrative and expository writing; the latter is more about mathematical argumentation. As you move around conferring and helping your students to get ready for the gallery walk, look for moments where you can facilitate development—moments where you can support more efficient strategies and students' justifications that are effective.

For the gallery walk, ask students to start at different places and choose three or four posters to focus on. Remind them to read carefully and then give each poster a few sticky notes, enough so that after about ten minutes all posters will have at least a few comments. Remind students that gallery walks should be quiet times so that all reviewers can read and think before commenting. This time should be taken seriously.

During the gallery walk it's important that you make comments on posters as well. It's important that students see you as a member of the community, not someone grading their papers, so look for moments and places where you can show them you are seriously trying to understand their thinking. Make your comments as a member of the audience, suggesting where more detail could be helpful to support understanding and commenting on interesting approaches. Raise questions that might push for generalization. As you move around, look for big ideas and strategies from the landscape. This is a nice time also to plan which pieces of work you will select for the congress.

Facilitating the Math Congress

Review the posters and choose a few that you can use for a discussion that will deepen understanding and support growth along the landscape of learning described in the overview. There is not necessarily one best plan for a congress. There are many different plans that might all be supportive of development.

You'll want to make this congress supportive of flexible conversion strategies. Have students share both an inch strategy (300-60) and a foot strategy (25-5). Discuss which is more efficient and whether both answers are right. If you had more than one group who also found the difference in yards, decide whether seeing this strategy would be beneficial to the rest of the students or distract them from their growing understanding of feet and inches. A window into one classroom follows as an example.

<table>
<tr><td>

Tech Tip

You might take pictures of students' work and project them onto a whiteboard or smart board. When different ideas come up in discussions, revisions can be drawn without having to mark on the student's work. Apps such as *Adobe Sketch* or *Explain Everything* can be useful tools for this.

</td></tr>
</table>

Inside One Classroom: A Portion of the Congress

Heather (the teacher): Sasha and Kashia, would you start us off? I've taken a picture of your poster and I'll project it up here. Come share with us about the model you used and what you discovered. When I conferred with you, you had originally written 25 over here, and 60 over there, right? And then you changed it. Tell us why.

Sasha: First we wrote 25 over here because it is a smaller number than 60, but then we remembered it was 25 feet, and the 60 was only 60 inches. A foot is much longer than an inch. When you measure with inches you might get a really big number because the inch is so small. Then we remembered that the FatMax was really 300 inches… a big number, so we moved the 300 over here.

Heather: So this is reminding me of what we talked about a couple of days ago. Turn and talk to your partner about what Sasha just said. Is it true that if you measure in inches you get a much bigger answer than if you measure in feet, but they are both right? 25 feet is the same length as 300 inches? *(After a few minutes of pair talk Heather resumes whole class discussion.)* Damian, what did you and Maia talk about?

Damian: We agree. 1 foot is the same as 12 inches. It's just the foot cut up into little pieces. So if you have a lot of little pieces the number is big. If you do it in feet the number is smaller, but it is the same thing. 300 inches is the same as 25 feet.

Heather: Ok, so Sasha and Kashia… After you realized that how did you find the difference between 60 inches and 300 inches?

Kashia: We used the open number line and took a jump of 40 to get to 100. Then we knew it was just 200 more. So, we got 240 inches.

Author's notes

Heather chooses two different strategies for discussion in order to engender discussion on the equivalence of lengths measured in feet and lengths measured in inches. She wants her children to come to understand that although the lengths have different answers, they are equal. By beginning with Sasha and Kashia she lays the foundation for the discussion.

Equivalence is now at the heart of the discussion, as well as the idea that longer units require less iteration.

Heather: Now if I'm right, Damian and Maia, when I looked at your poster you had a different answer. Tell us what you did.

Maia: We made the 60 inches into 5 feet. We knew the foot had 12 inches, so we kept adding on 12 inches. When we got to 60 we counted the 12s and we had 5. Then we thought 25 feet minus 5 feet is 20 feet. We just knew that part.

Heather: Ok, so let's turn and talk again. We have two very different strategies here and two different answers. Are they both right? *(Heather pauses a moment, and resumes when most conversations seem to have quieted.)*

Damian: If 60 inches is 5 feet, then I think 120 inches would be 10 feet….and 20 feet would be 120 plus 120.

Heather: Wow! That's interesting, Damian. Let me make a picture of your thinking on the open number line so we can discuss it. *(Heather draws the following:)*

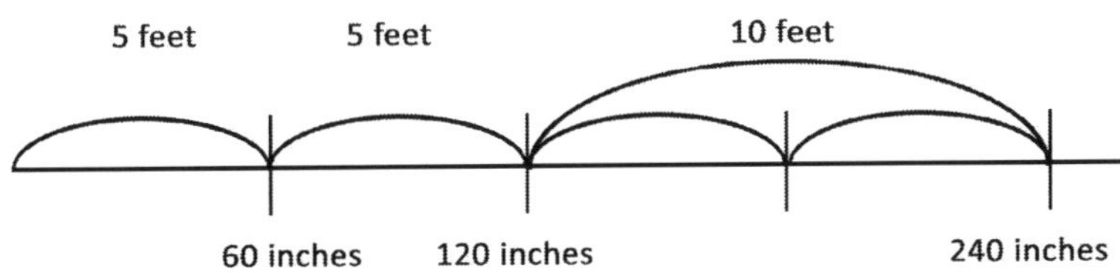

So let's all look at this picture. Is 20 feet the same length as 240 inches? Talk with your elbow partner…

Notice when Heather uses pair talk. She uses it strategically when she wants to promote reflection on a big idea. Children need time to make sense of ideas for themselves.

By representing Damian's idea on the open number line, Heather does two things: she provides a powerful representation for discussion so others can make sense of Damian's idea; but she is also implicitly demonstrating how mathematicians can use models as tools for thinking.

Minilesson: A String of Related Problems

This string is designed to continue helping students use flexible conversions to simplify addition and subtraction with units of measurement. As with previous strings, display children's strategies on an open number line as you go.

The String:
12 inches + 3 feet
36 inches – 1 foot
12 inches + 12 inches + 12 inches
300 inches – 10 feet
20 feet + 60 inches

Reflections on the Day

Math workshop began today with preparation for a gallery walk. As you moved around and conferred you may have noticed that more and more students are now starting to convert mentally. Each day you should see your children making progress on the landscape, but each child's pathway will likely be different. The lessons are not designed with one goal for all—one "it" for everyone to get. Each child should be learning, but most likely they are not all learning the same thing. Learning *is* development. Document the journey of each child on individual landscapes!

DAY FIVE

PLANS FOR THE TOOLBOX

<table>
<tr><td valign="top" width="33%">

Materials Needed

Tanisha and Tamika's Toolbox, Part Three (Appendix A)

Where to make the cuts? (Appendix D, one per pair of students, but have extras handy in case students change their plans as they work)

Pencils

Drawing paper or several sheets of copy paper for drafting

Blank Chart Paper for posters (sticky note style is best as it makes taping on the walls unnecessary)

Markers, Scissors, Paste Sticks or Scotch Tape

</td><td valign="top">

Today begins with another minilesson designed to support measurement conversions and subtraction to find the difference of two lengths. Then, a new context is developed: Tanisha and Tamika are building a toolbox and they have to come up with a plan for Tanisha's dad so he knows where to cut the boards. They have decided to build a box that is about 4 feet long by 3 feet wide by 2 feet high, with a cover. Mr. Arnold has bought six 10-foot long boards for the sides and some plywood for the frame, cover, and the bottom. Are the six 10-foot boards enough for the sides? Where shall they tell him to make the cuts?

Day Five Outline

Minilesson: A String of Related Problems

❖ Work on a string of related addition and subtraction problems using the open number line to record students' strategies.

Developing the Context

❖ Tell the story of how Tanisha and Tamika want to develop a plan for building the sides of a toolbox and how they have to determine what lengths to cut out of each 10-foot board for Tanisha's dad.

❖ Distribute Appendix D and ask students to work in pairs, making a plan. Have lots of extra copies of Appendix D and drawing paper handy so they can draft and change their plans as they work to find the most efficient use of the 6 planks.

Supporting the Investigation

❖ Confer with children as they work, noting the strategies they use. Support them to plan how to cut smaller pieces out of 10-foot lengths.

❖ As students finish, ask them to prepare a poster to convince others of their solutions and important things they have noticed along the way as they worked. These posters will be used on Day Six in a gallery walk and math congress.

</td></tr>
</table>

Minilesson: A String of Related Problems

This string is designed to keep familiarizing students with addition and subtraction of lengths. Children will need to convert back and forth but answers do not need to be in the same units as the addends. The purpose of the minilesson is to support flexible thinking, not a rule about converting to common units. For example, if a child thinks of 48 inches as 4 feet (using the problem above it) and says that 48 inches + 6 feet = 10 feet, accept this as correct as long as the community can justify it.

The String:

4 feet + 3 feet + _________ = 10 feet

10 feet − 6 feet =

4 feet + __________ = 10 feet

48 inches + __________ = 10 feet

3 feet + 3 feet + _______ = 10 feet

6 inches + 6 inches + 6 inches + 6 inches = ________

Developing the Context

Project a copy of Appendix A if you have the technology to do so, and read the next part of the story as you develop the context. If you don't have the technology, just read the story and show students the picture of the 1" by 6" by 10' board. As always, make the context come alive.

Pass out Appendix D and explain that all you know is that the girls want their box to be 4 feet by 3 feet by 2 feet and Mr. Arnold has already built a frame for it. Invite students to make plans for Mr. Arnold and to draw on the planks where they think the cuts should go. Remind them that they have drawing paper, too, and extra copies of the planks. DON'T provide rolls of adding paper. The point of this investigation is not for students to physically measure 4 feet; it is to consider how something 10 feet long can be cut into 4-foot, 3-foot, and 2-foot lengths.

Supporting the Investigation

As you move around conferring, take note of how children are planning. This investigation may take longer than the others as there is a lot to think about. Students may need help keeping track of their thinking, and how many pieces they have cut so far. Remind students of the dimensions Tanisha and Tamika decided on, and on the size of the boards that Mr. Arnold bought. Encourage them to draw out each side of the box and imagine what pieces they could cut out of the 10-foot boards. Some students may want to cut 4-foot, 3-foot, and 2-foot boards to match the three dimensions. Support children to notice that the boards have width as well as length. Since the width of one board is 6 inches, when two boards are next to each other the width becomes 1 foot. If the boards are laid lengthwise adjacent to each other, four boards will not only have length, but will also form the 2 feet of height (see Figure 8).

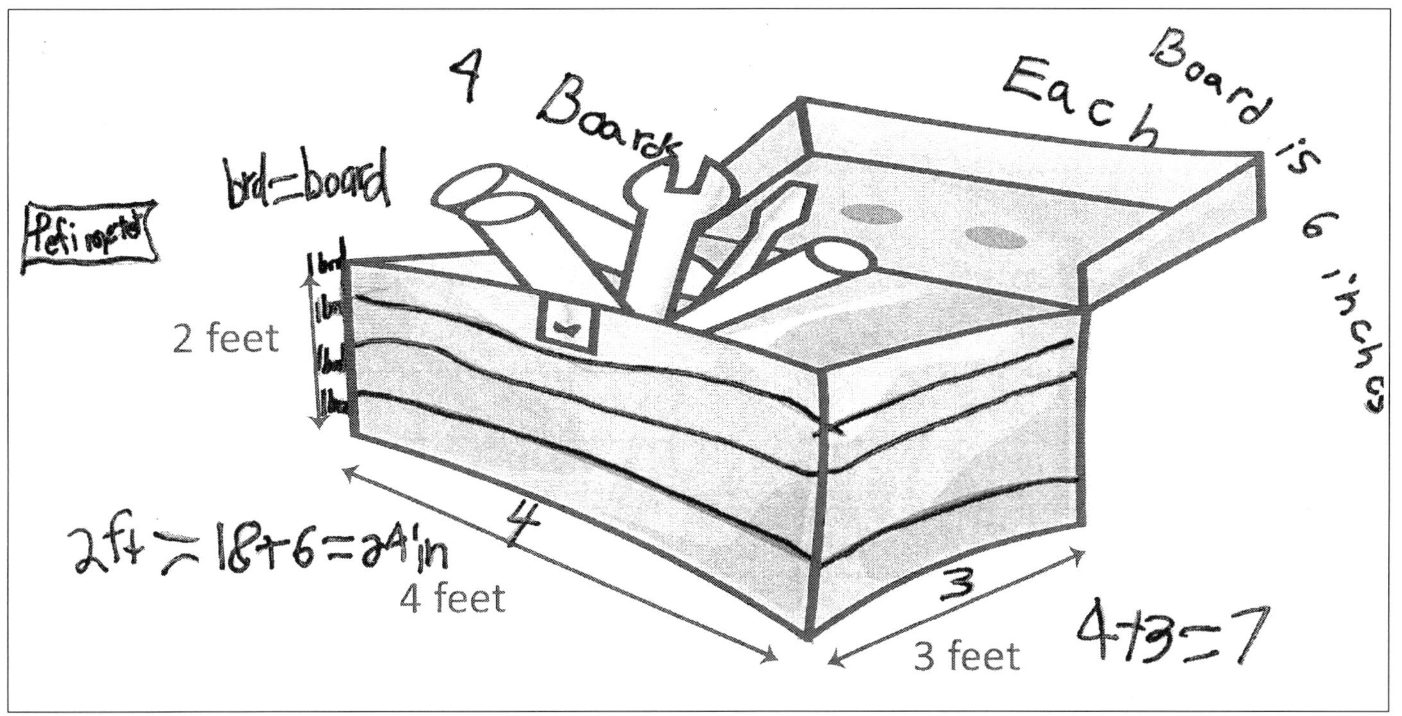

Figure 8. These students plan how they will lay the boards horizontally.

Alternately, students might want to cut pieces 2 feet tall and place them next to each other all the way around the box, "like a fence." These students will need 8 pieces for each of the 4 foot sides and 6 pieces for each of the 3 foot sides (see Figure 9).

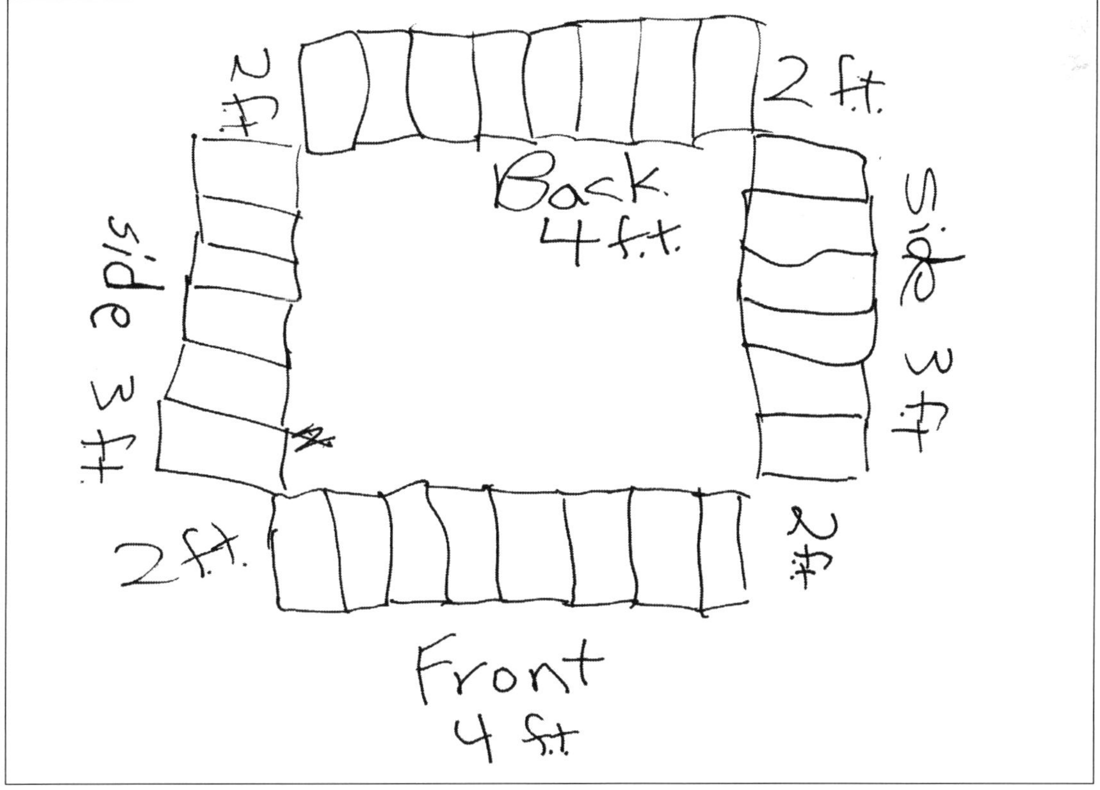

Figure 9. These students plan to cut 2-foot sections that will stand up vertically.

As you confer, note whether students are able to compute the total number of boards needed for the box and then make the cuts, or if they prefer to work one side at a time. Some students might benefit from labeling their pieces "front," "left," "right," or "back" to keep track of their work as they divide the boards. In particular, students who split the 10 feet into 3-4-3 may need a reminder that they also need to cut boards for the back of the toolbox. This is also a nice place to introduce some geometry terms. The box is a rectangular prism and each pair of its opposite sides are the same.

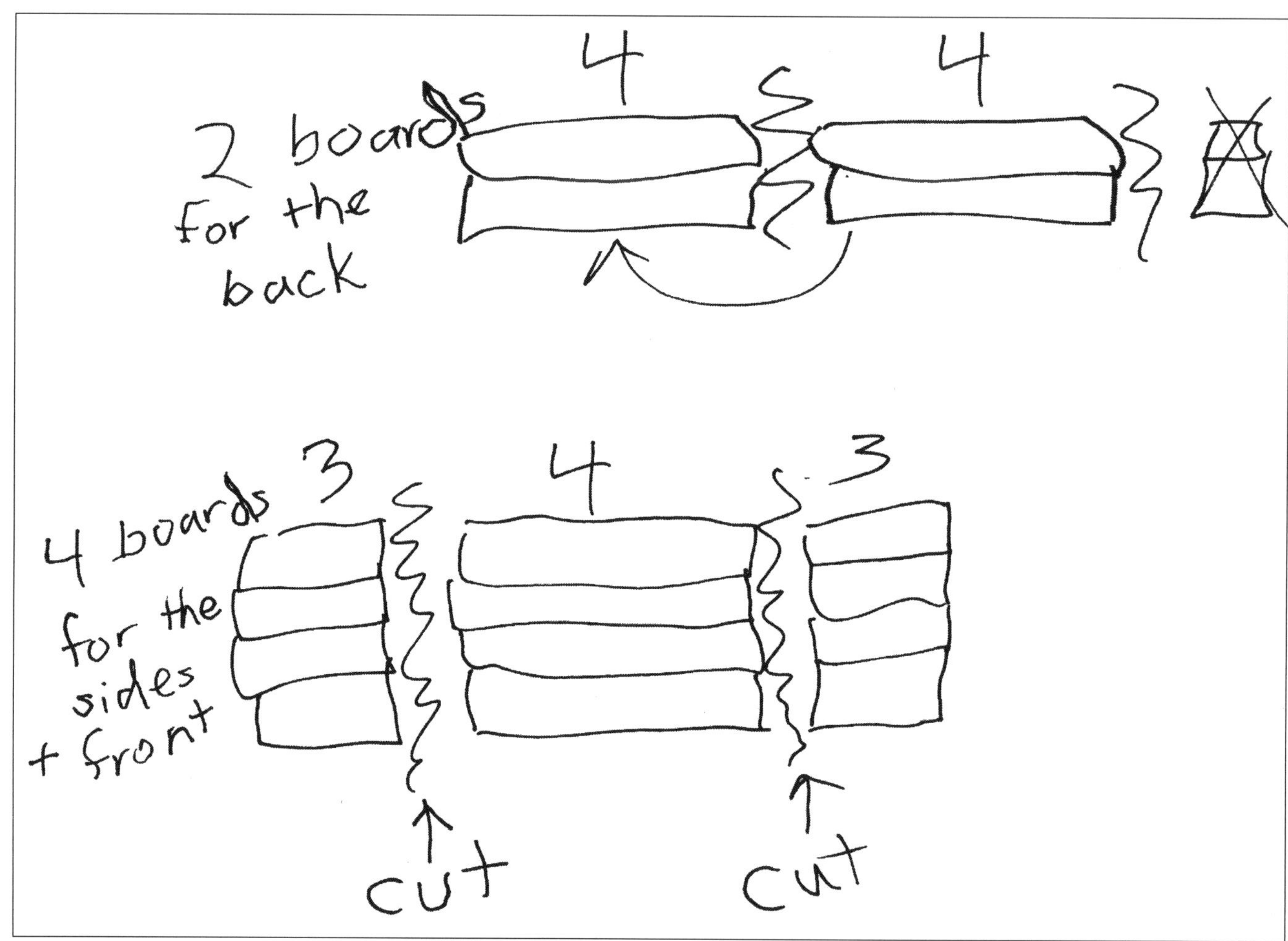

Figure 10. Students demonstrate the cuts they will make and how the boards can be used horizontally to form the four sides.

As students begin to mark the boards, take note of whether they are able to see that one cut stands for the boundary of two boards. You may find that some of the children draw two lines to separate a 4-foot board from a 3-foot board or draw a new cut past the edge of the board to begin the first piece. These students have not yet constructed the idea that a single line can simultaneously define two bounded areas. Ask them to imagine Mr. Arnold making the cuts. Will he need to cut the edge of one board and then the edge of the other? Or, once he makes a cut, will two pieces have a new edge? [Note: these groups are different from those that may have re-drawn the same line multiple times in an attempt to represent each of their pieces to scale. Be sure to clarify students' strategies when you confer with them.]

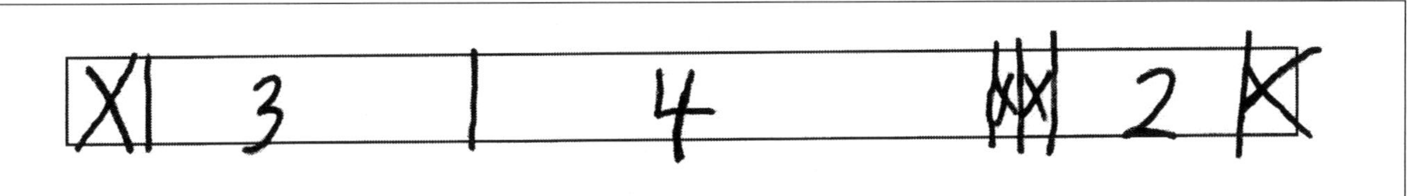

Figure 11. A student leaves gaps between the pieces and makes extra cuts.

Other students might mark out too many pieces. For an example, look at Figure 12 below. These students have marked out 4 feet, 3 feet, 4 feet, and then another 3 feet without considering the length remaining in the board, not realizing that their plan expects to get more than 14 feet out of a 10-foot board. The dialogue box below shows how a teacher conferred with the students whose work is shown below, helping them to see that the shorter lengths are subtracted from a whole.

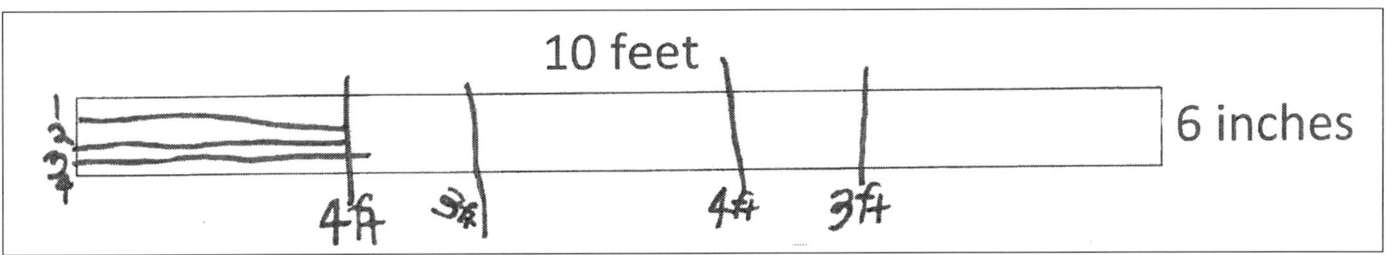

**Figure 12. This student does not consider that the boards being cut subtract length
from the total board or that the width of the board matters.**

Inside One Classroom: Conferring with Students at Work	

Heather (the teacher): What are you working on over here? This plan looks interesting!

Maia: We're all done. We knew we needed 4 and 3 and 4 and 3 for the different sides, so we cut them, see?

Sasha: And it takes 4 boards to build up to 2 feet tall, so we showed that here. *(He points to the left portion of the diagram.)*

Heather: Wow, so this one section is your whole plan? That's a lot of information in one spot!

Maia: Yep!

Heather: But wait a minute. You said you needed 4 boards to get the side tall enough, right? Are you cutting this piece of the board into 4 skinny pieces?

Sasha: I think so…

Maia: Wait, that doesn't work. It'd be too skinny.

Author's notes

Heather notices that these students are planning without attention to the dimensions of the board. They know the number and size of the pieces needed, but are not recognizing that the length and width also comprise the whole that they have to work with. They are not conserving the area.

Heather: The board is only 6 inches wide to begin with, remember? That's pretty short. Isn't that why you wanted 4 of them to stack up? We have 6 boards all together, so there are more you can use.

Sasha: Oh, so we have to cut the sides 4 times from different boards. We can do that.

Heather: Great! Let's do that. Okay, so pretend I'm Mr. Arnold going along this 10-foot board. First, you want me to cut after 4 feet. *(She mimes sawing the diagram.)* Okay, I did that. How long is the piece I have left?

Sasha: 10. Because we need 14 all together.

Heather: 10 left? I thought we started with a 10-foot board. That's what it said on the board when I bought it. It was originally 10 feet long and now we've cut off 4 feet.

Maia: Oh. Maybe it's 6? Cause 4 + 6 is 10.

Heather: Do you agree with that Sasha? If we cut 4 feet off of 10 feet there are 6 feet left?

Sasha: Oh, it has to be 10? I get it. The next one will be 3.

Heather: The next place I cut or the next leftover piece?

Sasha: Both! You had 6, so it's 3 and 3!

Maia: But what about the 4 for the back? It's not big enough for another 4?

Sasha: No, 4+3+3 used it all up.

Heather: Hmm... Let's think for a minute. We could get 4 and 3 and 3 from one board. I'm going to write that down here. *(Heather represents this on an open number line.)* But we do need more 4s. What would happen if the second cut had been 4 feet?

Maia: It's still 6 left, so... the last piece would be 2. So we could get 4 and 4 and 2 if we wanted. But how would we do the sides?

Sasha: Maybe we could make them out of the leftover 2s standing up? Or cut 3s in another board? Let's see.

When students understand that a single cut separates two boards and that lengths can be added and subtracted, their cuts will create sections that add up to 10 feet.

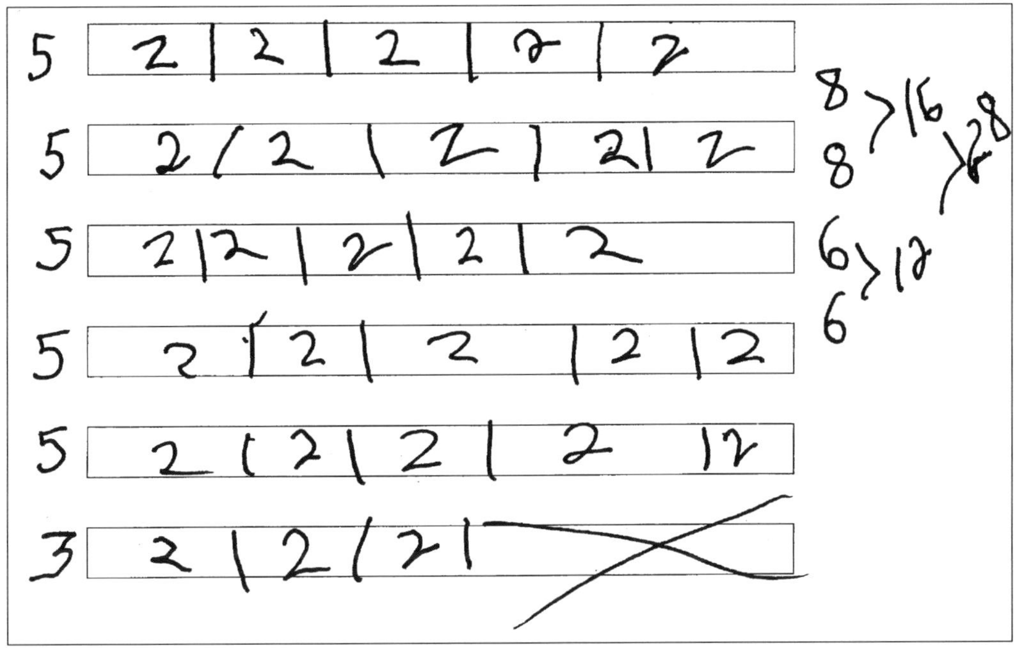

Figure 13. These students (whose work is also shown in Figure 9) cut five 2-foot boards from each 10-foot length. Regardless of the spacing of the cuts, they know when they have used up the total length.

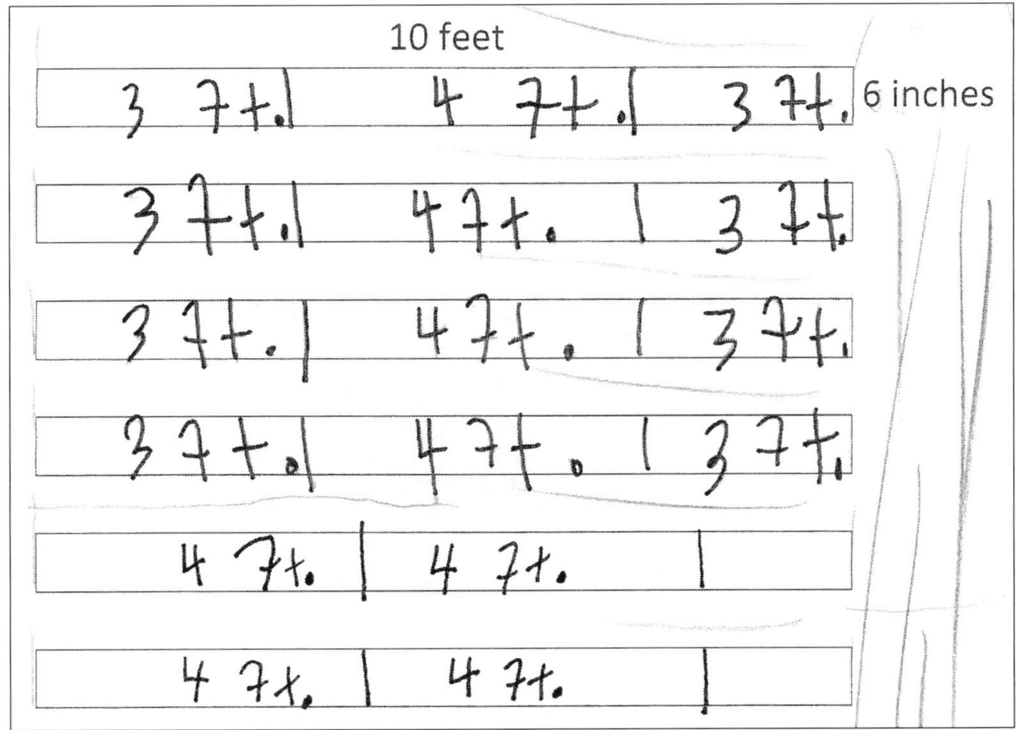

Figure 14. In this plan (similar to the examples shown in Figures 8 and 10), students attend to both the total length and relative spacing of the cuts.

Reflections on the Day

Math workshop began today with another minilesson. Are the minilessons causing children to look for relationships between numbers and use them in their computation? If so, that is wonderful. Remember that you can document children's growth on the landscape. And, even when this unit ends you can keep doing minilessons every day to continue working on measurement conversions and record children's progress further. The investigation today requires a lot of children as they plan their designs. As you moved around and conferred you may have noticed some children not able to keep track of all of the pieces. Figuring out a way to organize your thinking is an important part of doing mathematics. You probably found that supporting them to imagine each side of the box and to draw right on the picture of the box helped them to realize what was needed. Context helps children come to realize what they are doing and that is one of the primary reasons to use it. Without it, young mathematicians can get lost in a world of numbers and have nothing to hang their hats on!

DAY SIX

PRESENTING THE PLANS

Today begins with students adding finishing touches to posters from Day Five and a gallery walk ensues. After the gallery walk a math congress is held to discuss a few of the designs more deeply. The congress ends with a minilesson. Students work with a string of related problems designed to support addition and subtraction of lengths and converting from one measurement unit to another.

Day Six Outline

Facilitating the Gallery Walk

❖ Confer with children as they put finishing touches to their posters, asking them to consider the most important things they want to tell their audience about smart ways to cut the boards.

❖ Conduct a gallery walk to allow students time to reflect and comment on each other's posters on the investigation started on Day Five.

Facilitating the Math Congress

❖ Convene students at the meeting area to discuss a few important ideas about planning out the lengths to cut efficiently so as not to waste material.

Minilesson: A String of Related Problems

❖ Work on a string of related problems designed to encourage students to add and subtract lengths and to convert flexibly.

Materials Needed

Students' work from Day Five

Where to make the cuts? (Appendix D, extra copies)

Pencils

Drawing paper or several sheets of copy paper

Blank Chart Paper for posters (sticky note style is best as it makes taping on the walls unnecessary)

Markers

Facilitating the Gallery Walk

Ask students to return to the posters they began on Day Five, adding any finishing touches they desire. As they work, move around and confer, asking them to consider the most important things they want to tell their audience about smart ways to make the cuts so as not to waste materials. Suggest that all the students draw their plans to help their readers understand their designs. Remind them that it is not necessary to write about everything they did, but instead to concentrate on convincing their audience about the important things they discovered and want to defend. For example, if students have noticed how equivalent sections can be exchanged suggest they get that down with examples!

Facilitating the Math Congress

Review the posters and choose a few that you can use for a discussion that will deepen understanding and support growth along the landscape of learning described in the overview. There is not necessarily one best plan for a congress. There are many different ways to do this congress that might all be supportive of development, but the important math here that should get some focus is that equivalent pieces can be exchanged. For this reason you might want to use a plan that shows how five 2-foot pieces can be cut from 10-feet, and then use another that shows how the 10-foot plank could also be cut up into 4 + 3 + 3 or 4 + 4 + 2. By displaying several different plans side by side, you will provide students the opportunity to consider many equivalent ways to reach the same length. Not only can they subtract a smaller length from a longer one; students can also exchange equivalent pieces like 4+2 and 3+3.

Another important idea you may need to focus on in the congress is how just one cut makes two boards and how the pieces of each board combine to make the whole length. It is important for your young mathematicians to come to understand how smaller lengths can be cut from longer pieces. Finding the smaller lengths inside of the longer 10-foot piece supports children to consider the part/whole relations of length: lengths can be added and subtracted.

Minilesson: A String of Related Problems

This string is designed to keep familiarizing students with addition and subtraction of lengths. Children will need to convert back and forth between inches, feet, and yards, but answers do not need to be in the same units as the addends. In fact, an answer might even use two units such as "2 yards plus 1 foot more." Focus on supporting flexible thinking, not a rule about converting to common units.

The String:

48 inches + 3 feet + _________ = 10 feet

120 inches − 6 feet =

4 feet + __________ = 10 feet

36 inches + ___________ = 10 feet

3 feet + 1 yard + _______ = 10 feet

6 inches + 6 inches + ______ = 2 feet

Reflections on the Day

Today students shared their plans for building the toolbox and explored how six 10-foot boards could be enough for the sides using many different groupings. As children considered the pros and cons of the many plans they came up with, you were supporting them to consider how shorter lengths can be cut from longer lengths. This understanding builds the foundation for understanding addition and subtraction of lengths. As you moved into the minilesson at the end of the day, your children continued with opportunities to consider efficient ways to add and subtract lengths, as well as ways to determine the missing addend. Don't forget to document the growth and development you see!

DAY SEVEN

A NEW TOOL

Today begins with another minilesson designed to support addition and subtraction. Then a new investigation is introduced. The girls are given a new tool—a meter stick—with 100 centimeters marked on it. (They notice that the meter stick also has inches marked on the back side.) Tamika thinks the toolbox is longer than the meter stick and that the meter stick will fit nicely in the toolbox with their other tools. Students work to determine if Tamika is correct and to examine the difference in the two lengths.

Day Seven Outline

Minilesson: A String of Related Problems

❖ Work on a string of related addition and subtraction problems designed to support students' construction of constant difference.

Developing the Context

❖ Tell the story of the meter stick, using Appendix A. Then pass out Appendix E so that students can begin investigating the difference in the lengths.

❖ Emphasize to students that they are estimating—they are trying to get a close answer, but it might not be an exact number of centimeters.

Supporting the Investigation

❖ Confer with children as they work, noting the strategies they use to find the difference between the two lengths.

❖ As students finish, ask them to prepare a poster to convince others of their solutions and important things they have noticed along the way as they worked. These posters will be used on Day Eight in a gallery walk and congress.

Materials Needed

Tanisha and Tamika's ToolBox, Part Four
(Appendix A)

Which is longer?
(Appendix E, 1 copy per pair of students)

Meter sticks, yardsticks, and rulers
(one each per pair of students)

Adding machine paper

Pencils and Markers

Drawing paper or several sheets of copy paper

Blank Chart Paper for posters (sticky note style is best as it makes taping on the walls unnecessary)

Minilesson: A String of Related Problems

Begin the day in the meeting area, presenting the following addition and subtraction problems one at a time and recording student strategies on an open number line as shown in the dialogue box. Because constant difference is the focus of this minilesson, be sure to represent both the minuend and subtrahend as positions on the number line and the difference as the distance between them (see the teacher note after the dialogue box).

The String:

123 − 100

122 − 99

158 + 22

160 + 20

158 − 22

160 − 20

156 − 20

Behind the Numbers

The numbers in this string have been chosen to support the construction of constant difference, for example, 123 − 100 = 122 − 99. This strategy is an important subtraction strategy and it relates nicely to the context of the difference in lengths. When the difference stays the same, one can just slide the length along the number line to an easier place: 123 − 100 is a lot easier to do mentally than 122 - 99. Children often confuse compensation (which works nicely for addition) with constant difference. In this string they will discover, for example, that 158 + 22 = 160 + 20. If 2 is removed from the 22 and associated instead with the 158, the total stays the same (compensation). The students then try this with problems like 158 − 22, only to discover that 160 − 20 does not equal 158 − 22. This requires them to think deeply about subtraction. 158 − 20 − 2 = 158 − 2 − 20. The open number line is a good model to use for representation of these relationships.

Inside One Classroom: A Portion of the Minilesson

Heather (the teacher): Remember to show me with a "thumbs up" when you have had enough think time. Here's the first one: 123 − 100. I'm going to put these numbers on a number line. *(Several thumbs go up quickly. This is an easy problem for the group.)* Jamie? You had that quickly. What did you do?

Jamie: 23. I just knew it. You just need 23 more to get to 123.

Heather: Nice when you just know it, right? Who else thought that one was easy? *(All hands go up.)* So how about 122-99?

Paulo: I have a good way. I added 1 to get to 99 and then I needed 22 more. So the answer is 23.

Heather: The same answer that we got in the first problem? That's interesting. Does 122 − 99 = 123 − 100? I'm going to represent this on the same number line.

Author's notes

The representation of the addition and subtraction on the open number line supports students to consider the difference in the operations.

Heather: Turn to an elbow partner and talk about this. *(Heather gives some time for reflection and discussion and then resumes.)*

Paulo: I think they are. The lengths between the numbers are the same. It's like we just slid the problem over.

Heather: Let's see what happens with addition. *(She writes "158 + 22.")*

Kallie: I took 2 off the 22 and gave it to 158. 160 + 20 is 180.

(Heather draws an open number line and represents Kallie's strategy as follows:)

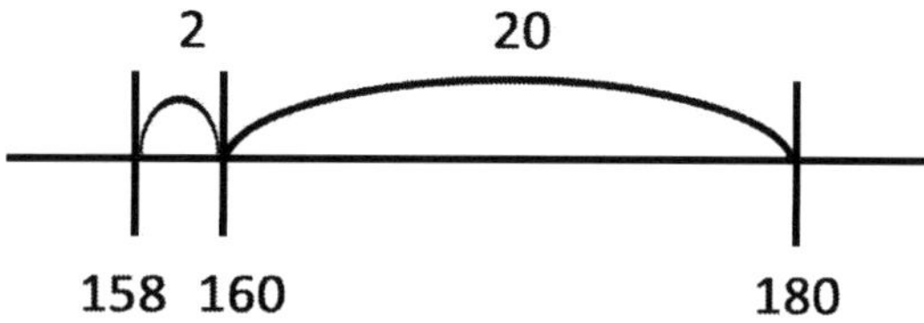

Heather: Hmm… Did anyone try to make it 160 + 24, adding 2 to both numbers? That's what Paulo said worked for the subtraction problem earlier.

Kallie: That wouldn't work. It would be too much.

Heather: Let's try your strategy with a subtraction problem, Kallie. What about 158 − 22. Does it work to make it 160 − 20?

Jamie: Oh I get it. It doesn't work for subtraction. Subtraction is like finding the difference… the length in between the numbers.

Heather draws what Jamie is trying to explain on the number line.

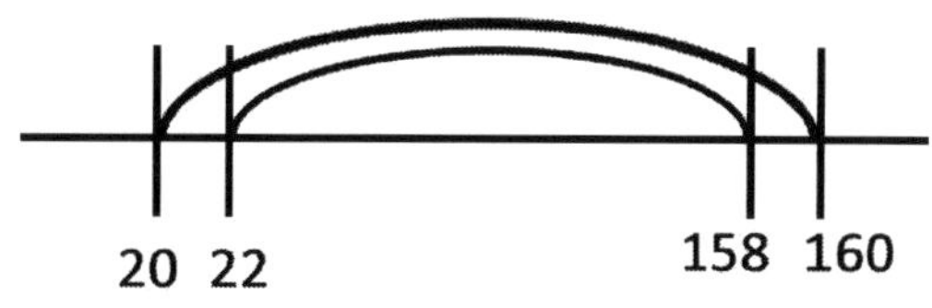

Paulo: The length between 158 and 22 is shorter than 160 and 20. To make it work for subtraction you have to keep the length the same and just slide it.

Kallie: Actually, I think we are using the 2 from the 22. It's just that we are subtracting, not adding. So if we take a 2 away first we get 156 - 20. So that's why we can't add it. We are subtracting it!

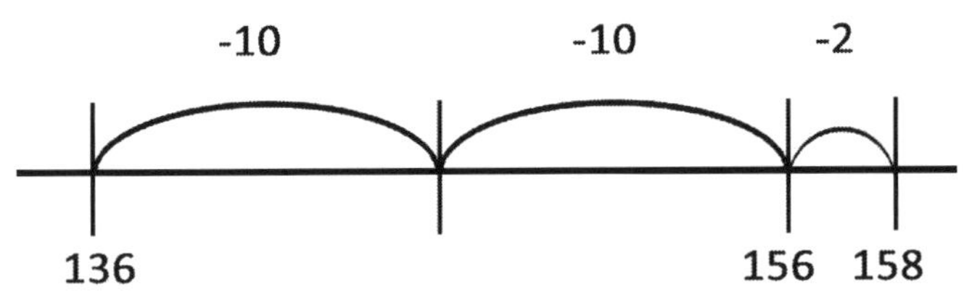

Now Kallie is connecting finding the difference with removal and Heather's final diagram helps the class visualize Kallie's thinking.

Developing the Context

Gather students in the meeting area to tell the story from Appendix A of how Tanisha and Tamika were given a new tool: a meter stick. Be sure to explain that the meter stick uses a different measurement system called the metric system. While 36 inches, 3 feet, and 1 yard all line up exactly, because they are part of the same system (customary U.S. units), the centimeters on the meter stick line up with the meter and might not match up exactly with the feet or inches. Students can still estimate, though. The goal here is for them to develop a sense of the magnitude of a meter and a centimeter. It is not to develop conversion rules. Focus on the following questions:

❖ About how many centimeters are equal to 4 feet?
❖ Is a length of 4 feet shorter or longer than the meter stick?
❖ Will the meter stick fit in the box?
❖ What is the difference between the meter stick and the 4 feet?

Once you ensure that students understand the questions, pass out copies of Appendix E and measuring tools to each partnership. Remind them that they have learned a lot about measuring already, and the strategies they have discovered may be helpful again today!

Supporting the Investigation

There are many ways students might approach this investigation. Some might begin by converting 4 feet to 48 inches, or 1 yard and 1 foot, because they are already familiar with these conversions. These groups will likely be stumped when they realize that, just as they don't know how to convert between feet and centimeters, they don't know how to convert from inches to centimeters either. With these children, encourage them to look to the meter stick for help. Maybe they will notice that 100 cm is equal to "just a little more than 39" or "almost 40" inches. They can mark either of these points on the double number line, and then see that 4 feet is about 8 or 9 inches beyond the end of the meter stick. Don't be afraid to challenge them with "How many centimeters is that?". The meter stick usually has inches on one side and centimeters on the other so they can examine the tool to help.

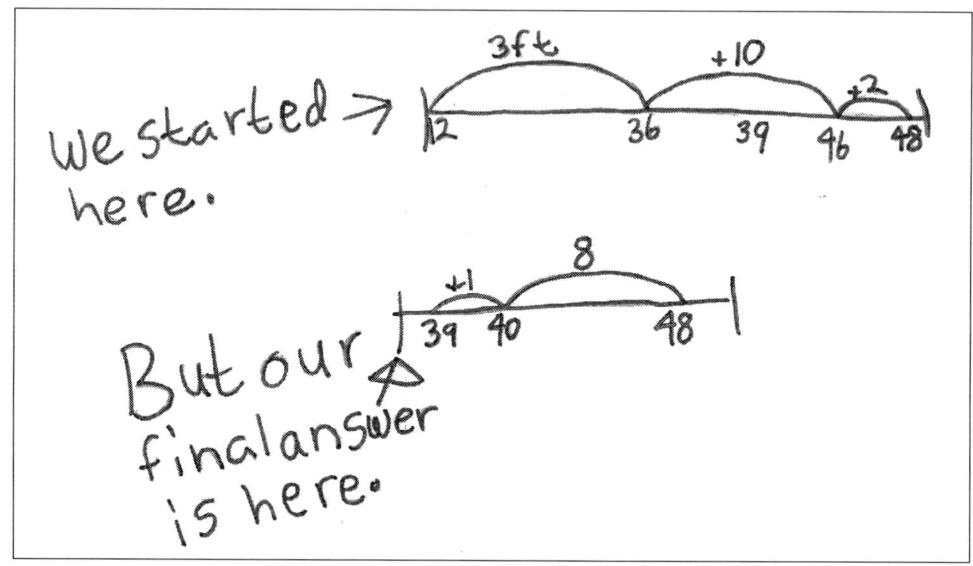

Figure 15. Students add on from 39 to reach 48.

Other students may want to measure out 4 feet, and then re-measure it with centimeters using the meter stick. Have adding machine paper available if students ask for it, but many students may simply line up the ruler and yardstick to make 4 feet to compare with the meter stick. They should be able to determine the difference in centimeters and inches from the extra portion of the ruler or yardstick. If students choose this route, encourage them to represent their work with a number line when they make their posters. These groups are likely to be the most precise, and it will be interesting to compare their work with their peers who may have just estimated.

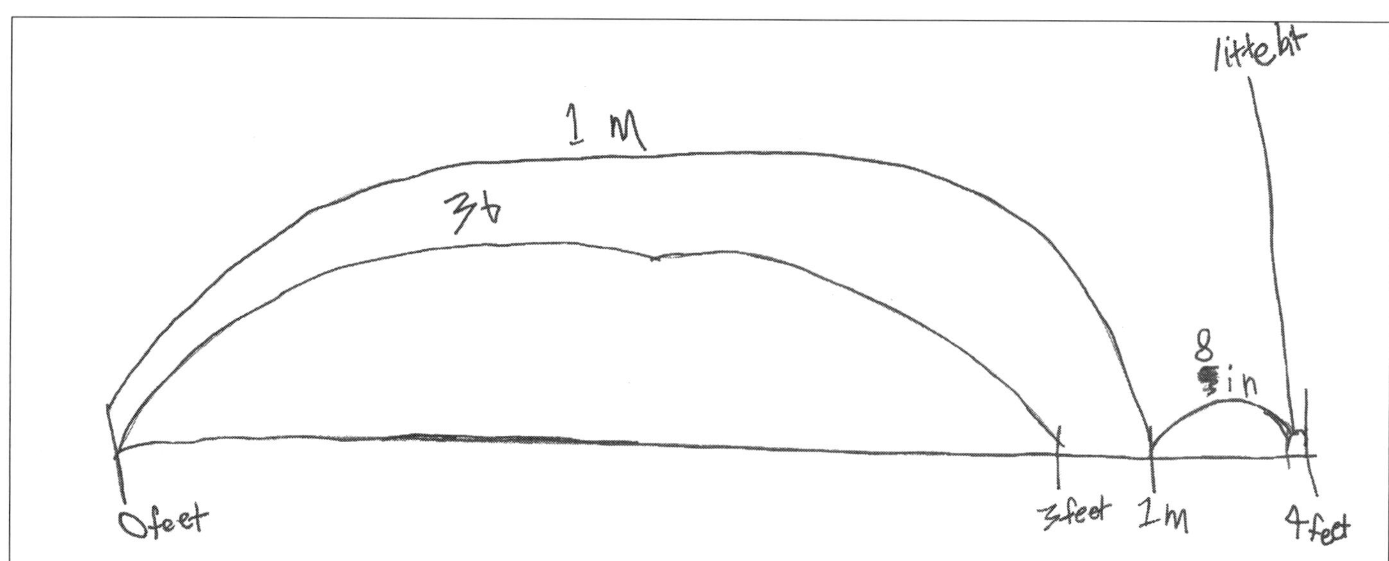

**Figure 16. These students used the meterstick, ruler, and yardstick,
and then recorded the results on an open number line.**

Once they have the difference in inches, some students may make conjectures about the relationship between centimeters and inches. Based on the two sides of the meter stick, some students might notice that there are a little more than 2 centimeters in an inch, or a little less than 3 centimeters. (The exact conversion is actually 2.54 centimeters to an inch.) Following this reasoning, students may determine that 9 inches are between 18 and 27 centimeters. This is excellent work! Although their answers are not yet accurate, the students are reasoning proportionally and skip counting in ways that will support their future mathematical development. The dialogue box below shows how a teacher might confer with students using this strategy.

<table>
<tr><td colspan="2">

Inside One Classroom: A Portion of the Minilesson

</td></tr>
<tr><td>

Heather (the teacher): Hi Kallie and Jamie, how's it going over here?

Jamie: We saw that it's 39 inches in a meter, so it's 9 more to get to 48 inches. We drew it, and we're ready to do a poster.

Heather: That's nice work that I see on your number line! That's definitely poster material. But before you start, I wonder how many centimeters it is. Have you figured that out too?

Jamie: Oh.

Kallie: It's not that hard. One inch is 2 centimeters—see on the meter stick?—so 9 inches is a double, too… so, 18 centimeters.

Heather: Nice thinking! We can use the relationship to go from inches to centimeters pretty quickly. But how did you figure out that there were 2 centimeters in each inch?

Kallie: I flipped over the meter stick and used my finger. See?

Heather: Oh yeah, I do see it's about 2. But let me just check something. *(Heather takes the meter stick and puts her finger on 9 inches. Flipping the meter stick, she is pointing to 23 centimeters.)* Huh. That's strange. I got 23 centimeters when I started from 9 inches.

Jamie: Maybe it wasn't exactly 2.

Kallie: That could be. It must have been a little bit bigger. Maybe… 2 ½ centimeters?

Heather: That's an interesting guess. I look forward to reading about all of this on your poster. It's such a puzzle!

</td><td>

Author's notes

Heather celebrates the students' work, which shows they have internalized the number line model and are even able to take jumps of 2 cm and 1 inch at the same time. She then helps students check their work by looking at a larger distance. Over repeated iterations of the inches, their relationship with centimeters becomes clearer. It's not important that students derive the exact equivalence (they certainly won't arrive at 2.54 independently at this stage!), but by estimating and checking they are exploring powerful big ideas about equivalence and they are developing a sense of the magnitude of a meter in relation to the foot and the yard, and the magnitude of inches in relation to centimeters.

</td></tr>
</table>

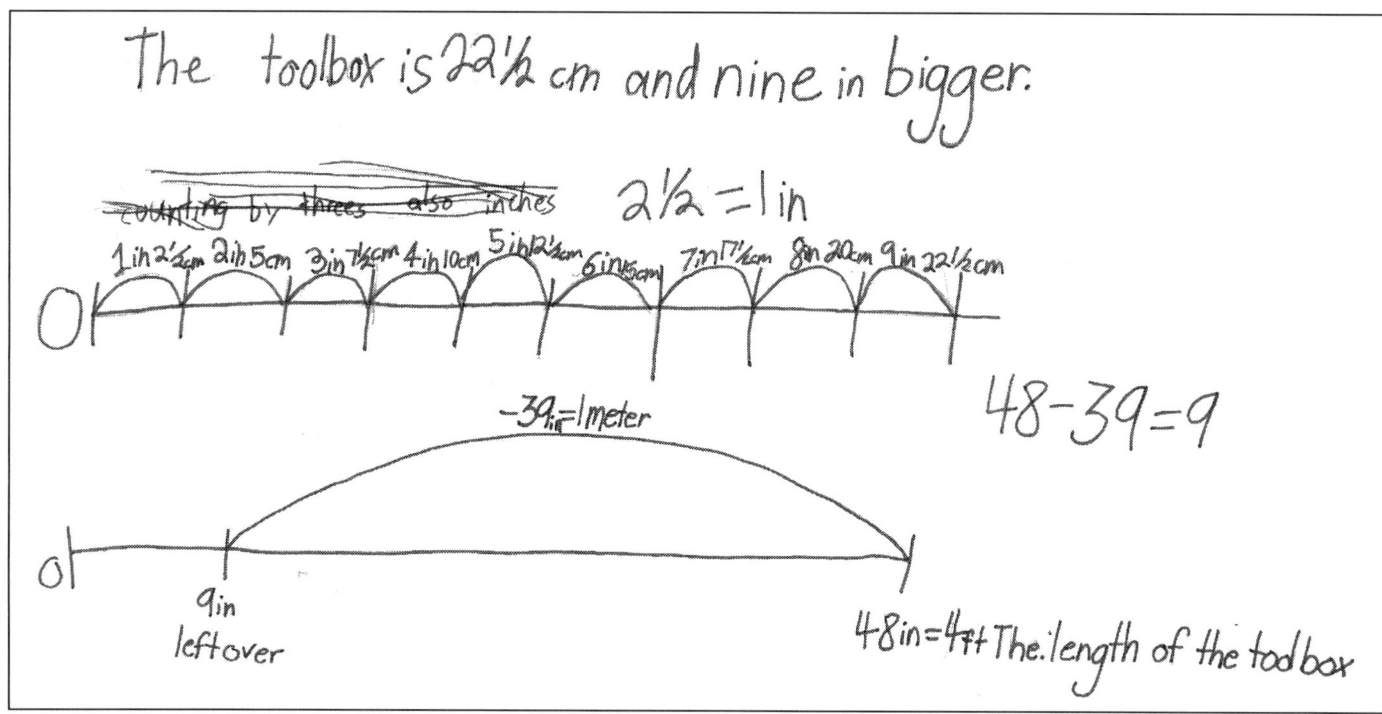

Figure 17. Students originally skip counted by 3 cm at a time, but revised to count 2 ½ cm for each inch.

Reflections on the Day

Today students began with a minilesson challenging them to think deeply about number relationships in addition and subtraction. Next, they were asked to transfer their knowledge of measurement with inches, feet, and yards to a new context: the metric system. Working with measuring tools and modeling their thinking on open number lines, many students were likely comfortable using subtraction to find the distance, or difference, between two lengths. Recognizing that centimeters are smaller than inches, some students may even have searched for a proportional relationship between the two systems. Take a moment to note how far your students have already progressed during this unit!

DAY EIGHT

WHAT'S THE DIFFERENCE?

Materials Needed

Students' work from Day Seven

Pencils and Markers

Drawing paper or several sheets of copy paper

Sticky notes (about three per child)

Blank Chart Paper for posters (sticky note style is best as it makes taping on the walls unnecessary)

Today begins with another minilesson to revisit the ideas about constant difference explored on Day Seven. Next, students participate in a gallery walk to examine and respond to each other's work. Finally, students convene for a math congress to discuss their strategies for comparing centimeters, meters, inches, and feet and finding the difference between 1 meter and 4 feet.

Day Eight Outline

Minilesson: A String of Related Problems

❖ Work on a string of related addition and subtraction problems designed to support students' construction of constant difference.

Facilitating the Gallery Walk

❖ Confer with children as they put finishing touches to their posters, asking them to consider the most important things they want to tell their audience about the difference between 1 meter and 4 feet.
❖ Conduct a Gallery Walk to allow students time to reflect and comment on each other's posters from the investigation started on Day Seven.

Facilitating the Math Congress

❖ Convene students at the meeting area to discuss a few important ideas about their strategies and models for finding the difference between two numbers.

Minilesson: A String of Related Problems

Convene the students in the meeting area to begin the day with another string of addition and subtraction problems. As on Day Seven, be sure to represent the subtraction problems as finding the distance between the minuend and subtrahend so that students will be able to see the constant differences between related problems.

The String:

$$138 - 100$$
$$137 - 99$$
$$249 + 39$$
$$249 - 39$$
$$240 - 30$$
$$250 - 40$$

Facilitating the Gallery Walk

Ask students to return to the posters they began on Day Seven, adding any finishing touches they desire. As they work, move around and confer, asking them to consider the most important things they want to tell their audience about the relationship between centimeters and feet or inches. Remind them that it is not necessary to write about everything they did, but instead to concentrate on convincing their audience about the important things they discovered and want to defend.

At this point in the unit, students should be becoming more skilled at writing comments. Figures 18-20 show examples of helpful and specific student comments.

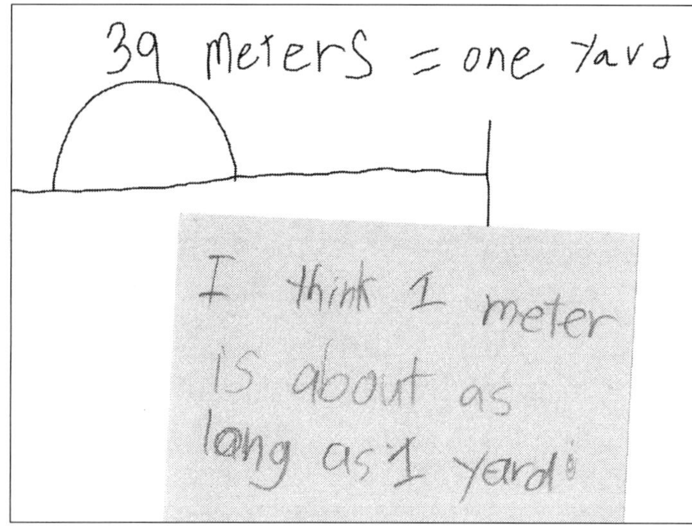

Figure 18.

"[I disagree.] I think 1 meter is about as long as 1 yard."

Figure 19.

"Wow. Why is my answer not the same?"

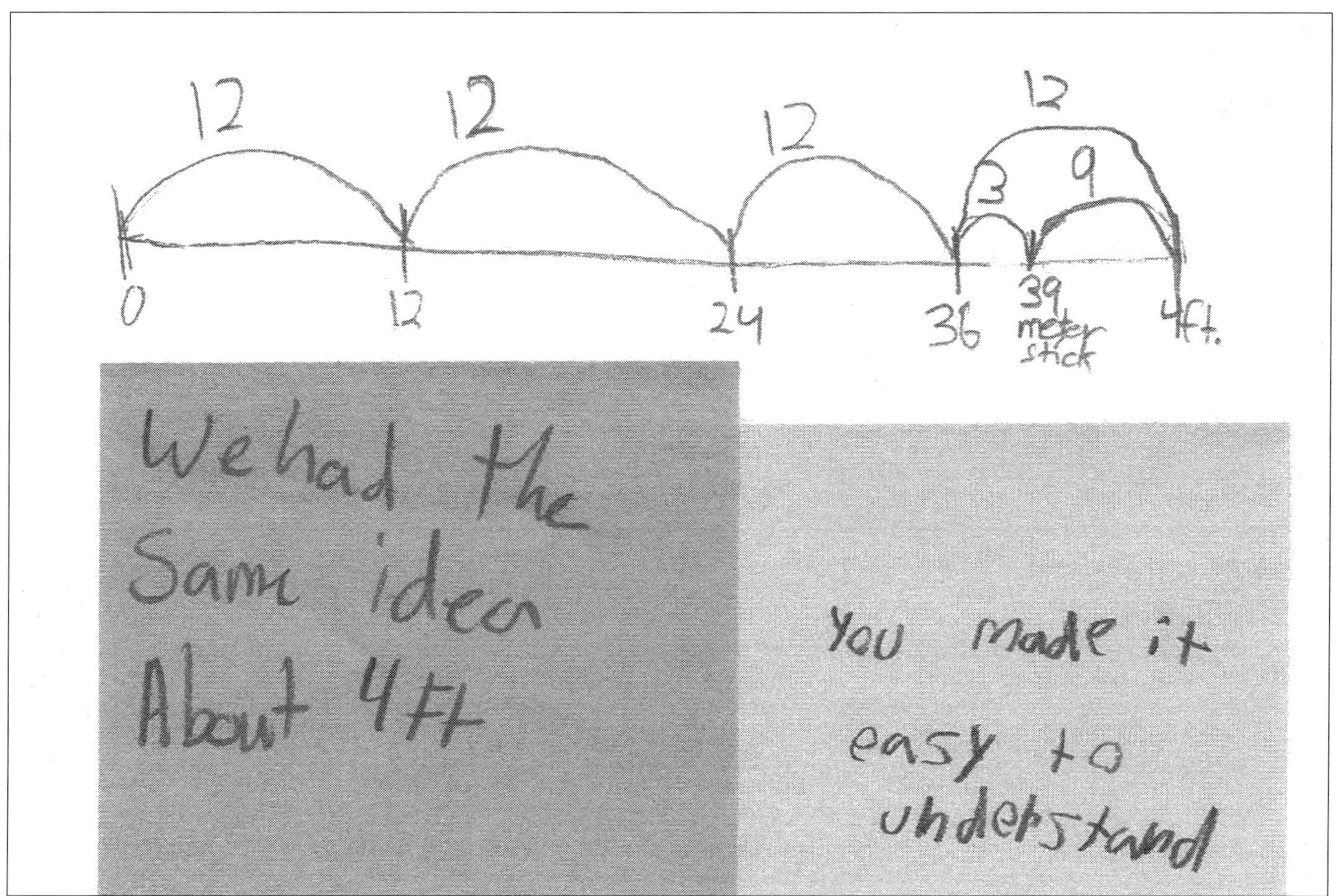

Figure 20. "We had the same idea about 4 ft." and "You made it easy to understand."

Facilitating the Math Congress

Review the posters and choose a few that you can use for a discussion that will deepen understanding and support growth along the landscape of learning described in the overview. By this point in the unit, you should have a good idea of where your students are. Would many in the group benefit from a few more opportunities to see (or present) how to find the difference between two lengths on an open number line? Are they considering pieces of small units or using a number line to compare centimeters and inches? Which posters generated the most interest or puzzlement during the gallery walk? There is not necessarily one best plan for a congress. There are many different plans that might all be supportive of development. Use the Landscape of Learning provided in the Overview as you plan. It is helpful to look at each piece of work and consider how it might steer a conversation. Which big ideas or strategies would be supportive of growth for your students right now?

Heather (the teacher): I'd like to start today with a comment I noticed in the gallery walk. Paulo, you wrote a note on Seung-Min and Maia's poster. "We got 9 on the number line. Are you sure it's only 8?" That's such a specific question, I think it will help us start a good conversation! Seung-Min and Maia, can you start us off by explaining your work?

Maia: Well, we laid out the meterstick next to the yardstick and we needed the ruler too. So we looked on the ruler and it was a little past 8.

Heather: Do other people see what Maia is saying here? *(Other students seem confused and shake their heads.)* Maia, why don't you lay them out again on the floor here? And Seung-Min can show us where you found the eight and a half.

Maia: See, at first we had the yardstick and the meterstick, but the yardstick was only 3 feet. Then we added the ruler to make 4 feet.

Seung-Min: We put the ruler with the 12 inches next to the yardstick so it started counting in the empty part. The meter stick was partway past the 8, so that's how we knew it was 8 and a little bit.

Heather: Oh, I think I see now. Show me with your thumb if you can see what Maia and Seung-Min were thinking here. *(Most thumbs go up.)* So let's hear from Paulo and Dante to compare.

Dante: You can see our number line on our poster right here. The meter was 39 inches. We saw that on the back. So to get to 48 inches for 4 feet we needed 9 more. That's how we got 9.

Heather: So now we have two different answers, huh? Turn to an elbow partner and talk about this. Is it 9 inches, or is it 8 and a little bit? *(Heather gives some time for reflection and discussion and then resumes.)*

Sasha: We got 9 too, but now I think maybe it's a little less than 9. When I look at the meterstick now, I see it was a tiny bit more than 39, so we missed that part.

Paulo: Oh, that could be. We didn't notice the extra part.

Heather: So, Sasha and Paulo, you're saying that if the meter stick is actually a little bit longer than 39 inches, then the distance to 48 would be a little bit shorter? That's interesting! What do other people think about this idea? Could "a little less than 9" be the same as Maia and Seung-Min's answer of "8 and a little bit"?

Author's notes

Heather begins with a comment from the gallery walk to reinforce that this feedback is a meaningful part of the mathematical conversation in the classroom.

By measuring carefully, Maia and Seung-Min have discovered the need for an even smaller unit—a part of an inch.

Now Heather has also succeeded in helping students ponder subtraction relationships. If the smaller number increases, the distance between the two numbers will decrease. And could "8 and a little bit" be the same as "a little less than 9"? These are rich discussion topics for students to ponder.

Reflections on the Day

After a brief minilesson on addition and subtraction strategies, students had another opportunity today to share and discuss their growing expertise in linear measurement. Most students will be more accurate in their measurements now, and may be able to fluently convert between inches and feet. How are they transferring their knowledge about larger and smaller units to the new context of the metric system? How are they beginning to use the open number line as a tool for new thinking? Be sure to document their journeys!

DAY NINE

ABOUT HOW LONG?

Measuring the Classroom (Appendix F, 1 copy per pair of students)

Measuring tools (meter sticks, yardsticks, and rulers

Pencils and Markers

Drawing paper or several sheets of copy paper

Today students have an opportunity to estimate length of objects around the room and then to measure to see how close their estimate was. They are invited to use their knowledge of different units to select an appropriate tool that will keep the iterations manageable and the answer precise. The day concludes with a minilesson connecting the addition and subtraction work students have been doing with conversion between meters and centimeters.

Day Nine Outline

Minilesson: A String of Related Problems

❖ Work on a string of addition and subtraction problems designed to introduce simple conversions between centimeters and meters.

Developing the Context

❖ Explain that students have an opportunity today to estimate and then measure the lengths of different objects around the room to see how close their estimates were.

❖ Encourage discussion and reflection on how the size of the units will affect the exactness of the measurements and ask them to consider that goal when they choose a tool for each object.

Supporting the Investigation

❖ Confer with children as they work, noting the strategies they use to estimate and whether they have a general sense of how a centimeter, inch, foot, yard, and meter compare in size.

❖ As students measure move around and confer and note the strategies they are using and the tools they choose for each case.

Minilesson: A String of Related Problems

Begin the day in the meeting area, presenting the following addition and subtraction problems and recording student strategies on a double open number line to show the conversions, if for example students convert meters to centimeters.

The String:

123 cm − 1 meter

122cm − 99 cm

198 cm + 2 cm

198 cm + 22 cm

152 cm − 122 cm

160 cm − 1 meter

160 cm − 99 cm

Behind the Numbers

The numbers in this string have been chosen to support the use of the metric system as a helpful model for addition and subtraction. The model simplifies all of the problems as the children at this point will likely be able to understand that the meter can be found inside of longer centimeter measurements. As you work with the string, represent students' strategies on a double number line as shown below with meters on the top and centimeters on the bottom.

Developing the Context

Gather students in the meeting area, and reflect with them about the learning that has been going on during this unit, saying something like the following.

> *Wow, over the last several days we've learned a lot about measurement tools, haven't we? A few days ago, some of you just looked at a meter stick and instantly knew it was smaller than 4 feet. That's some good estimating! I thought it would be fun if we estimate the lengths of other things around the classroom. Like this whiteboard, for example. How long do you think it is?*

Begin the discussion with the length of a large object, something like a whiteboard, a dimension of the classroom, or even the length of a piece of chart paper that might be measured in any of the units students have been using. As students share estimates, you'll likely note that they use a variety of units. Encourage discussion around the numbers and units. Could an estimate of 55 inches and another of 4 feet both be close to the actual length? What if someone else suggests 150 centimeters? After all estimates are put forth and discussed, measure the object under discussion and see how close the estimates were.

Explain that today students are going to estimate the length of a number of objects, and then check by measuring. As a class, list six or seven objects you'd like to know the lengths of and make a chart like the example shown below. Ensure that some objects are smaller (requiring inches or centimeters for precision) and others are larger (and therefore more efficiently measured with larger units). If the class selects any rectangles, such as a table, clarify which edge you are talking about. You may even want to mark the edge with masking tape so that all students are clear which length is to be measured. The following table is just an example of the types of objects you might select.

Object	Estimated Length	Measured Length
Whiteboard (long side)		
Textbook (short side)		
Student desk or table (short side)		
Length of the classroom		
Unsharpened pencil		
Width of the door		
Width of the window		

Pass out copies of Appendix F so that students can record the objects to be measured and make their initial estimates. All students should measure the same objects so that they are able to compare their results during the congress tomorrow. [Note: Depending on your students, you may choose to pre-select the objects children will measure and fill them in before copying Appendix F.] Since each partnership is sharing one chart, remind students to discuss which units and tools seem like a good fit for the size before estimating a number. Whichever unit they use to estimate will be the unit they measure in!

Supporting the Investigation

After five or ten minutes, once students are finalizing their estimates, distribute measuring tools and ask students to measure the actual lengths to compare with their estimates. As you circulate, ensure that students are measuring carefully, with no gaps or overlaps, and keeping track of their results as they go. Students also might not realize that they should stay within one measuring system for each object. If students are measuring in feet or yards, any extra section should be measured in inches (not centimeters), whereas any extra section for a measurement in meters should be given in centimeters. Explain to students that staying in one system at a time will help them keep the measurements more precise. Remind them how tricky it was to find the exact difference between the meter stick and 4 feet!

Reflections on the Day

The day began with a minilesson to remind students of the relationship between centimeters and meters and to support them to use these relationships to help with addition and subtraction. Afterwards, students used their knowledge of units of measurement to select appropriate units, make estimates, and measure distances precisely. Probably, many students are now comfortable exchanging equivalent measurements when it is convenient and decomposing and switching units when necessary. Remember to document each student's growth using the landscape!

DAY TEN

REFLECTING ON MEASUREMENTS

Students' work from Day Nine

Sticky notes (about three per partnership)

Bulletin board paper, prepared with student work

Reflection prompts

Pencils and Markers

Today students hold a final math congress to discuss which units of measurement are the best in different contexts. After comparing answers and sharing their insights, students reflect on their work throughout the unit and provide reflections they will share with the class and their community on a "learning scroll."

Day Ten Outline

Facilitating the Math Congress

❖ Give students sticky notes to share some of their measurements from Day Nine on a large class chart.
❖ Discuss the different units and tools that students used and their estimation strategies.

Constructing the Learning Scroll

❖ Convene students at the meeting area to discuss how their ideas about measurement changed over the course of the last two weeks.

Facilitating the Math Congress

Gather students in the meeting area, and display a new version of the measurement chart from Day Nine, this time with a column for each unit as shown below. With their work in front of them, ask each team to fill out a few sticky notes with measurements they found and then place the post-its in the appropriate box of the chart. [Note: The purpose here is not for students to convert and fill in each box. Just have them place the measurements they did in the appropriate columns to match the tools they used.] When every object has at least one measurement and all groups have placed at least one sticky note, reconvene the group for a congress discussion of their measurements.

Object	Measured length in centimeters	Measured length in meters	Measured length in inches	Measured length in feet	Measured length in yards
Whiteboard (long side)					
Textbook (short side)					
Student desk or table (short side)					
Length of the classroom					
Unsharpened pencil					
Width of the door					
Width of the window					

There are several ways you might structure the conversation about the measurement chart. Perhaps students are concerned that some of the boxes are empty. If so, you might begin by asking whether it would really make sense to measure a pencil (or some other small object) in yards. Ask students to share the reason they selected centimeters or inches for the small objects. Maybe some students used more than one tool and most of the boxes are filled, in which case you might ask students which is the "best" measurement for the object. There are no right answers to this question, but many good arguments! Students may say that using yards is best because it's an efficient unit to measure long objects like the width of the door or the length of the classroom, or that using inches is best because it allows them to compare with other objects measured in inches. Students may say they chose centimeters and meters because "it's easier to work with 100 than 36" or that they chose feet because "it's a good size to picture in my head." All of these arguments are helping students deepen their understanding of the available standard units within our measuring systems and to take into consideration the relationship between the size of the unit and the number of iterations needed when choosing a tool.

As you wrap up the final math congress of this unit, your students may be curious what happened to Tanisha and Tamika. If you wish, read the optional ending to Tanisha and Tamika's story which hints at the investigations students may encounter in a third grade unit featuring the same characters: *Building Benches and Measuring Tools.*

Building the Learning Scroll

A learning scroll is a class display—a sort of " socio-historical" wall—documenting the progression of the unit, children's questions, the important ideas constructed over the past two weeks, samples of students' work, and descriptions of their strategies and ideas, including anecdotes of how students' thinking changed over time. It is a document of the progression and emergence of learning over the past two weeks. By making this display available, you allow your students to revisit and reflect on all the wonderful ideas and strategies that emerged as they worked throughout the unit. Developmentally, second graders will need you to scaffold some of this reflection work, but will also be able to partner in identifying and describing their thoughts and strategies.

In preparation for today's work, use a roll of chart paper and cut out a long length sufficient to cover a bulletin board or a display area in a hallway. Curl and staple the two ends, making a small roll on each end. Staple or tape the scroll to the area to be covered. On the left begin with a picture of the Stanley FatMax 25 with a few samples of children's work. Selectively pick key pieces of children's work from the ten days of the unit and include these on a pathway from left to right, leaving plenty of blank space for anecdotes and explanations. You can also include pictures of the students and use a speech bubble to show insights they had along the way, or even ideas they may have had that were eventually disproved. This is a nice place to show the students' estimates from the work they discussed today as well, with their work alongside showing their calculations of the difference between their estimate and the actual length.

Today, ask students to reflect on the learning they did as they worked to measure and find the difference between lengths. You may want to provide templates with the empty speech bubbles with prompts like "At first I thought…" "Then I realized…" and "A good strategy was…" Attach these student explanations to the learning scroll. Wherever you can, show the developmental emergence of ideas on the landscape in the Overview. Display the scroll somewhere that students, and hopefully also the wider school community, will be able to revisit and reflect on their learning in the weeks to come.

Reflections on the Unit

The word geometry stems from the words geo (earth) and metric (to measure). In this unit, children have had many opportunities to explore and measure the different lengths and the classroom around them. They have grown in their understanding of the open number line, a powerful model that can be used to reason about addition and subtraction and to compare measurements using different units and even different systems of measurement.

Note the landscape depicted on the graphic in the Overview. Children began by comparing the values they produced when using different units to measure the same distance. They used a double number line to represent equivalent measurements such as 36 inches and 1 yard. Next students began to compare different lengths, finding the difference between two measuring tapes and later between distances in different measuring systems. When asked to cut 10-foot boards into pieces, students were pushed to deepen their understanding of part/whole integration and to note how lengths can be added and subtracted. By the end of the unit, you will probably notice many students choosing appropriate units, exchanging known equivalent measurements when it is helpful, and decomposing or switching units when needed.

Just as Tanisha and Tamika seek out tools that will help them measure, plan, and construct their ideas, students in this unit have developed powerful ideas about measurement and built or strengthened their understanding of how models can be tools for thinking. These models will support them as they take on exciting new projects in the months and years to come.

Tanisha and Tamika's Toolbox

Tanisha and Tamika are best friends. They live next door to each other and have played together every day since they were babies. Now they are in the same second grade class together! Mrs. Washington is their teacher and she is always finding fun math problems for them to do. "Investigations," Mrs. Washington calls them.

In the beginning of the year, Tanisha and Tamika helped Mrs. Washington build a blueprint with measurements on it so she could measure and make signs for a school art show. Tamika thought of the idea. She brought a roll of adding machine paper to school, and all of the kids measured the art papers with connecting cubes and then they turned the roll of paper into a measuring strip with all their measurements marked on it.

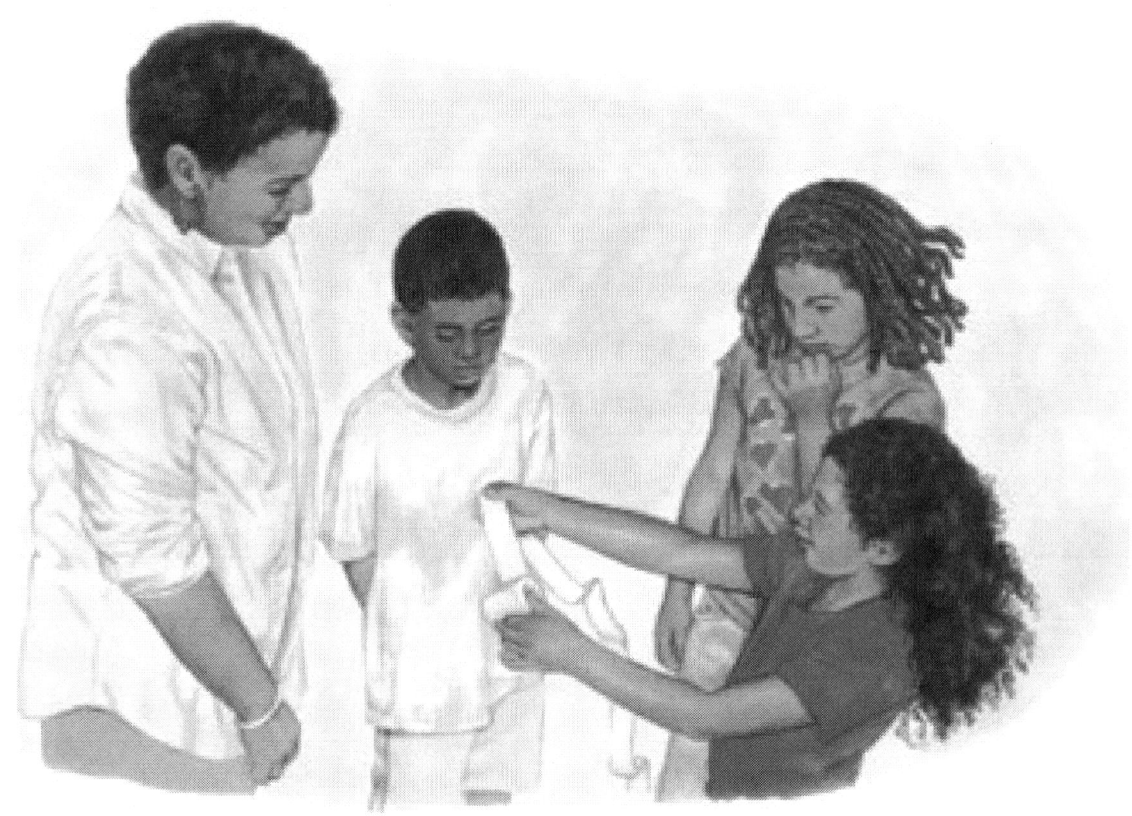

Tanisha's dad, Mr. Arnold, is a carpenter and when he learned about what Tanisha and Tamika had done, he got out his carpenter's tape measure to show it to them. "It sounds like you are making a measuring tool like mine," he said. He had a lot of numbers on his tape measure! It was called a Stanley FatMax 25.

"Why does it say '25' on it?" Tanisha asked him.

"It is 25 feet long," explained her dad.

"Wow, that's really long!" thought Tanisha. "I wonder how long that is?" She told Tamika about the Stanley FatMax 25 and they decided to investigate.

to begin investigation on Day One

on Day Three

The Stanley FatMax 25 is only one of Tanisha's dad's tools. They are so fascinating! Her dad wears them on a big black tool belt with his name on it. Each tool has a place on the belt. Hooks, straps, pouches and pockets hold the tools in place. He carries hammers, pliers, nails, screws, screw drivers, chisels, and levels. The Stanley FatMax 25 goes in the top center pouch.

At home, Mr. Arnold has even more tools that he stores in a toolbox.

More than anything, Tanisha wanted tools, too. If she had tools she could build things! She could even build a toolbox with Tamika and they could paint it red like her dad's.

Tanisha begged and begged her dad to get her a tool belt with some tools, but he would always just smile whenever she brought it up. Then one day her dad came home from work with a belt for her! She couldn't believe it! He had listened!

She immediately ran next door to show the tool belt to Tamika. They were both excited, particularly when they saw all of the tools in it! It even had a measuring tool like the Stanley FatMax 25, only smaller. The girls pulled it out and saw that the numbers on it went from 1 to 60—60 inches! They wondered how their measuring tape compared to the Stanley FatMax 25. Which was longer?

"60 is a bigger number than 25," thought Tanisha. Was her tape measure even longer than the FatMax?

to begin investigation on Day Three

Tanisha and Tamika began to think of the toolbox they would like to build and how they would paint it shiny red.

Tanisha told her dad about their plan and he said he would buy some boards for them. If they did the measuring, he would use his table saw to cut the boards for them and help them build it.

"How big should we make it?" Tamika asked Tanisha.

"Let's make a big one," said Tanisha. "Let's make it 4 feet long."

"Ok," said Tamika, "and let's make the width about 3 feet, and the height about 2 feet."

Tanisha told her dad what they had decided and the next day he went to the lumberyard and bought some 1 inch by 6 inch boards that were each 10 feet long. He also bought a sheet of plywood to cut out the bottom and the cover and he bought some metal corner pieces to hold the four sides together and some metal hinges for the cover.

"And now you have a real investigation to do," he said with a smile when he returned. "I'll make the bottom and the top out of the plywood for you, and I bought these metal corner pieces to hold the sides together, but I'll need you to make a plan of how to cut the boards for the rest of the box. You want the box to be 2 feet high and sides to be about 4 feet by 3 feet, right? How many pieces will we need, and where should I cut? Think about this carefully and be efficient. There might be wood left for other projects if you plan well."

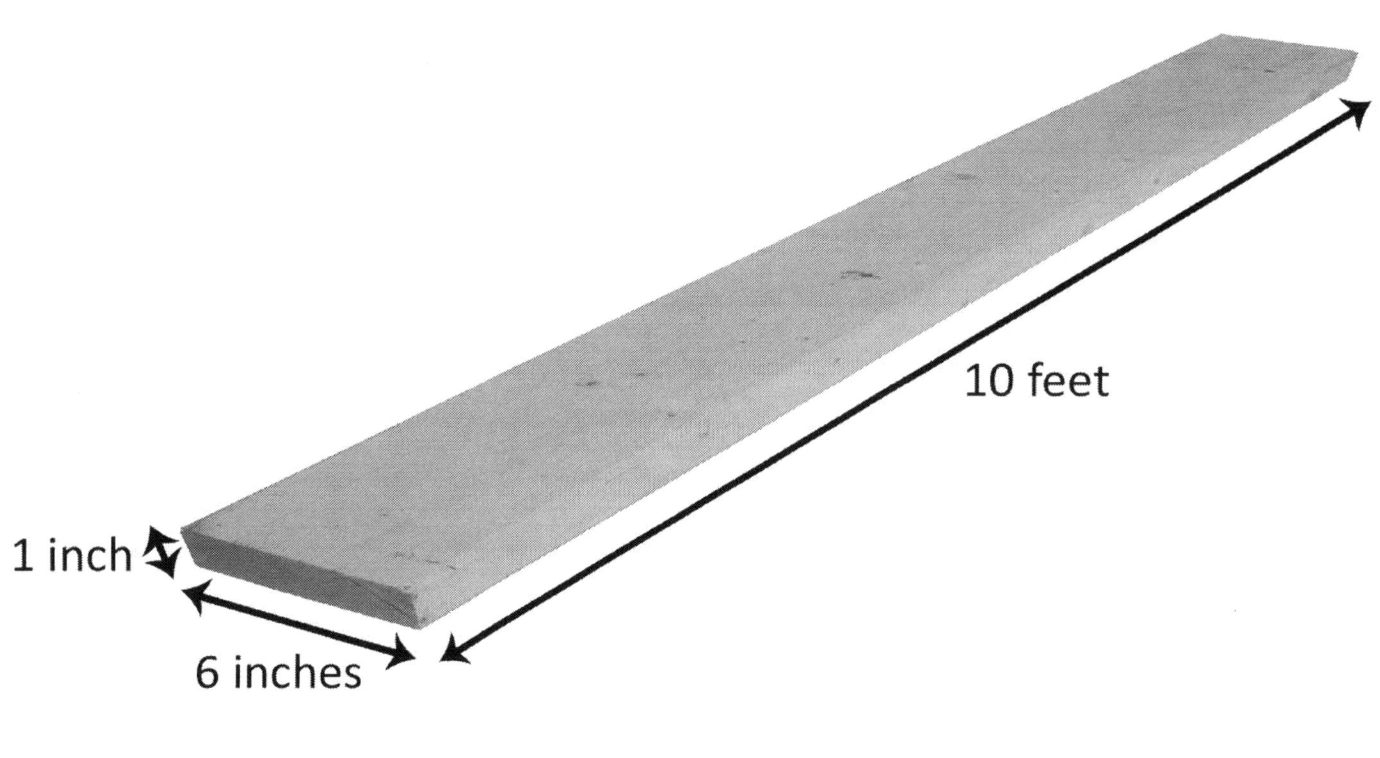

to begin investigation on Day Five

on Day Seven

It took a while, but finally the girls thought they had a nice plan. Tanisha's dad used the plan to cut the boards and it worked! After he cut the wood for them he helped them nail and screw the boards in place and soon the girls had a beautiful toolbox, which they painted shiny red.

"Now we need some more tools to put in our toolbox," said Tanisha.

"Let's have a drop-off place under the big tree in the back of your house," suggested Tamika. "We could have a sign for people to bring by old tools they don't want any more. We'll put out jars for leftover screws and nails too. We'll see what people bring, but I bet we'll get a lot of tools!"

The next day, the girls set everything up under the tree and during the day various neighbors stopped by and dropped old tools off. One neighbor brought a meter stick and Tamika asked him what it was for. He explained that he preferred to measure with a different system than inches, feet, and yards. He explained that he used a metric system. He showed them how his meter stick had 100 small centimeters on it instead of inches.

"Let's try it out," said Tamika. I think the toolbox is longer than the meter stick, so it should fit in our toolbox. But I think we have another investigation to do. I'll cut out a strip of paper from our roll. I'll make it exactly 4 feet like the tool box. Let's see if we can figure out how many centimeters long it is using this meter stick.

to begin investigation on Day Seven

on Day Ten (optional)

The red toolbox was such a success! Tanisha and Tamika enjoyed learning how to use all of their tools and continued to measure and build many new projects. With Mr. Arnold's help, they soon became skillful carpenters. The next year, in third grade, they even helped to build benches for their classroom!

How long is 25 feet?

How many inches?

How many yards?

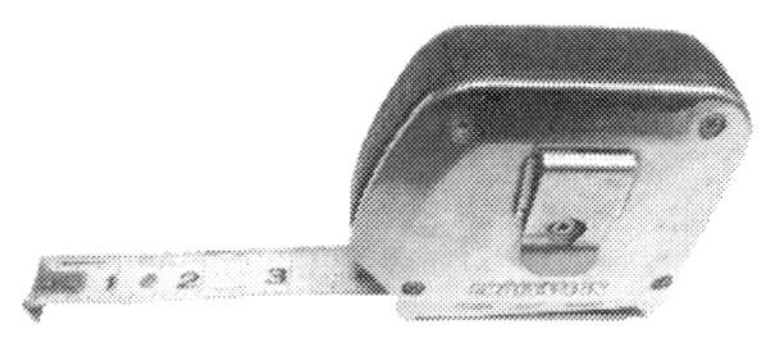

60 inches

25 feet

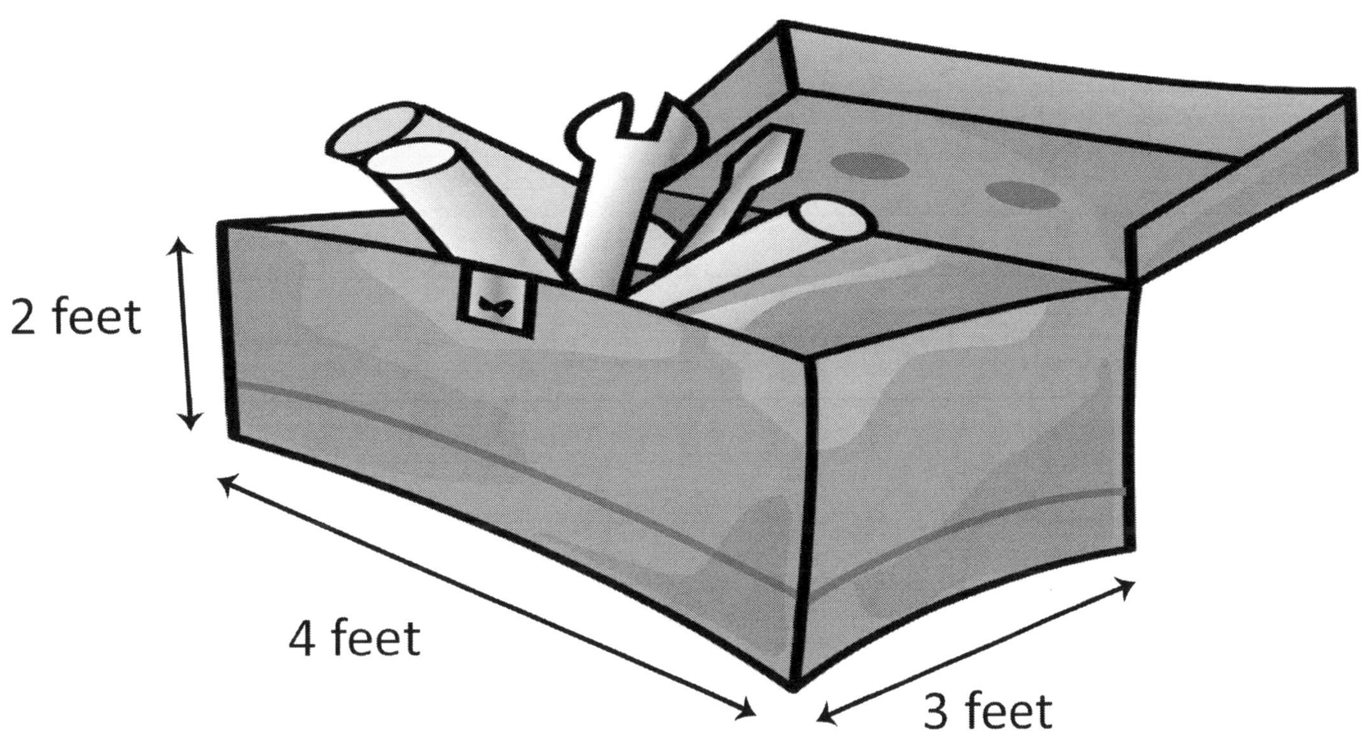

How many pieces of wood will be needed?

Where should the cuts go?

10 feet

6 inches

Was Tamika right? Is 4 feet longer than the meter stick?

What is the difference between 1 meter and 4 feet?

Object	Estimated Length	Measured Length

Made in the USA
Columbia, SC
23 June 2018